World War II: A Very Short Introduction

VERY SHORT INTRODUCTIONS are for anyone wanting a stimulating and accessible way in to a new subject. They are written by experts, and have been translated into more than 40 different languages.

The Series began in 1995, and now covers a wide variety of topics in every discipline. The VSI library now contains over 350 volumes—a Very Short Introduction to everything from Psychology and Philosophy of Science to American History and Relativity—and continues to grow in every subject area.

Very Short Introductions available now:

ACCOUNTING Christopher Nobes
ADVERTISING Winston Fletcher
AFRICAN AMERICAN RELIGION
    Eddie S. Glaude Jr.
AFRICAN HISTORY John Parker and
    Richard Rathbone
AFRICAN RELIGIONS Jacob K. Olupona
AGNOSTICISM Robin Le Poidevin
ALEXANDER THE GREAT
    Hugh Bowden
AMERICAN HISTORY Paul S. Boyer
AMERICAN IMMIGRATION
    David A. Gerber
AMERICAN LEGAL HISTORY
    G. Edward White
AMERICAN POLITICAL PARTIES
    AND ELECTIONS L. Sandy Maisel
AMERICAN POLITICS Richard M. Valelly
THE AMERICAN PRESIDENCY
    Charles O. Jones
AMERICAN SLAVERY
    Heather Andrea Williams
ANAESTHESIA Aidan O'Donnell
ANARCHISM Colin Ward
ANCIENT EGYPT Ian Shaw
ANCIENT EGYPTIAN ART AND
    ARCHITECTURE Christina Riggs
ANCIENT GREECE Paul Cartledge
THE ANCIENT NEAR EAST
    Amanda H. Podany
ANCIENT PHILOSOPHY Julia Annas
ANCIENT WARFARE Harry Sidebottom
ANGELS David Albert Jones
ANGLICANISM Mark Chapman

THE ANGLO-SAXON AGE John Blair
THE ANIMAL KINGDOM
    Peter Holland
ANIMAL RIGHTS David DeGrazia
THE ANTARCTIC Klaus Dodds
ANTISEMITISM Steven Beller
ANXIETY Daniel Freeman and
    Jason Freeman
THE APOCRYPHAL GOSPELS
    Paul Foster
ARCHAEOLOGY Paul Bahn
ARCHITECTURE Andrew Ballantyne
ARISTOCRACY William Doyle
ARISTOTLE Jonathan Barnes
ART HISTORY Dana Arnold
ART THEORY Cynthia Freeland
ASTROBIOLOGY David C. Catling
ATHEISM Julian Baggini
AUGUSTINE Henry Chadwick
AUSTRALIA Kenneth Morgan
AUTISM Uta Frith
THE AVANT GARDE David Cottington
THE AZTECS David Carrasco
BACTERIA Sebastian G. B. Amyes
BARTHES Jonathan Culler
THE BEATS David Sterritt
BEAUTY Roger Scruton
BESTSELLERS John Sutherland
THE BIBLE John Riches
BIBLICAL ARCHAEOLOGY Eric H. Cline
BIOGRAPHY Hermione Lee
THE BLUES Elijah Wald
THE BOOK OF MORMON
    Terryl Givens

BORDERS Alexander C. Diener and
    Joshua Hagen
THE BRAIN Michael O'Shea
THE BRITISH CONSTITUTION
    Martin Loughlin
THE BRITISH EMPIRE Ashley Jackson
BRITISH POLITICS Anthony Wright
BUDDHA Michael Carrithers
BUDDHISM Damien Keown
BUDDHIST ETHICS Damien Keown
CANCER Nicholas James
CAPITALISM James Fulcher
CATHOLICISM Gerald O'Collins
CAUSATION Stephen Mumford and
    Rani Lill Anjum
THE CELL Terence Allen and
    Graham Cowling
THE CELTS Barry Cunliffe
CHAOS Leonard Smith
CHILDREN'S LITERATURE
    Kimberley Reynolds
CHINESE LITERATURE Sabina Knight
CHOICE THEORY Michael Allingham
CHRISTIAN ART Beth Williamson
CHRISTIAN ETHICS D. Stephen Long
CHRISTIANITY Linda Woodhead
CITIZENSHIP Richard Bellamy
CIVIL ENGINEERING David Muir Wood
CLASSICAL LITERATURE William Allan
CLASSICAL MYTHOLOGY Helen Morales
CLASSICS Mary Beard and John Henderson
CLAUSEWITZ Michael Howard
CLIMATE Mark Maslin
THE COLD WAR Robert McMahon
COLONIAL AMERICA Alan Taylor
COLONIAL LATIN AMERICAN
    LITERATURE Rolena Adorno
COMEDY Matthew Bevis
COMMUNISM Leslie Holmes
COMPLEXITY John H. Holland
THE COMPUTER Darrel Ince
CONFUCIANISM Daniel K. Gardner
THE CONQUISTADORS
    Matthew Restall and
    Felipe Fernández-Armesto
CONSCIENCE Paul Strohm
CONSCIOUSNESS Susan Blackmore
CONTEMPORARY ART Julian Stallabrass
CONTEMPORARY FICTION
    Robert Eaglestone
CONTINENTAL PHILOSOPHY
    Simon Critchley
CORAL REEFS Charles Sheppard
COSMOLOGY Peter Coles
CRITICAL THEORY Stephen Eric Bronner
THE CRUSADES Christopher Tyerman
CRYPTOGRAPHY Fred Piper and
    Sean Murphy
THE CULTURAL
    REVOLUTION Richard Curt Kraus
DADA AND SURREALISM
    David Hopkins
DARWIN Jonathan Howard
THE DEAD SEA SCROLLS Timothy Lim
DEMOCRACY Bernard Crick
DERRIDA Simon Glendinning
DESCARTES Tom Sorell
DESERTS Nick Middleton
DESIGN John Heskett
DEVELOPMENTAL BIOLOGY
    Lewis Wolpert
THE DEVIL Darren Oldridge
DIASPORA Kevin Kenny
DICTIONARIES Lynda Mugglestone
DINOSAURS David Norman
DIPLOMACY Joseph M. Siracusa
DOCUMENTARY FILM
    Patricia Aufderheide
DREAMING J. Allan Hobson
DRUGS Leslie Iversen
DRUIDS Barry Cunliffe
EARLY MUSIC Thomas Forrest Kelly
THE EARTH Martin Redfern
ECONOMICS Partha Dasgupta
EDUCATION Gary Thomas
EGYPTIAN MYTH Geraldine Pinch
EIGHTEENTH-CENTURY
    BRITAIN Paul Langford
THE ELEMENTS Philip Ball
EMOTION Dylan Evans
EMPIRE Stephen Howe
ENGELS Terrell Carver
ENGINEERING David Blockley
ENGLISH LITERATURE Jonathan Bate
ENTREPRENEURSHIP Paul Westhead
    and Mike Wright
ENVIRONMENTAL ECONOMICS
    Stephen Smith
EPIDEMIOLOGY Rodolfo Saracci
ETHICS Simon Blackburn

ETHNOMUSICOLOGY Timothy Rice
THE ETRUSCANS Christopher Smith
THE EUROPEAN UNION John Pinder
    and Simon Usherwood
EVOLUTION Brian and
    Deborah Charlesworth
EXISTENTIALISM Thomas Flynn
THE EYE Michael Land
FAMILY LAW Jonathan Herring
FASCISM Kevin Passmore
FASHION Rebecca Arnold
FEMINISM Margaret Walters
FILM Michael Wood
FILM MUSIC Kathryn Kalinak
THE FIRST WORLD WAR
    Michael Howard
FOLK MUSIC Mark Slobin
FOOD John Krebs
FORENSIC PSYCHOLOGY
    David Canter
FORENSIC SCIENCE Jim Fraser
FOSSILS Keith Thomson
FOUCAULT Gary Gutting
FRACTALS Kenneth Falconer
FREE SPEECH Nigel Warburton
FREE WILL Thomas Pink
FRENCH LITERATURE John D. Lyons
THE FRENCH REVOLUTION
    William Doyle
FREUD Anthony Storr
FUNDAMENTALISM Malise Ruthven
GALAXIES John Gribbin
GALILEO Stillman Drake
GAME THEORY Ken Binmore
GANDHI Bhikhu Parekh
GENES Jonathan Slack
GENIUS Andrew Robinson
GEOGRAPHY John Matthews and
    David Herbert
GEOPOLITICS Klaus Dodds
GERMAN LITERATURE Nicholas Boyle
GERMAN PHILOSOPHY Andrew Bowie
GLOBAL CATASTROPHES Bill McGuire
GLOBAL ECONOMIC HISTORY
    Robert C. Allen
GLOBAL WARMING Mark Maslin
GLOBALIZATION Manfred Steger
GOD John Bowker
THE GOTHIC Nick Groom
GOVERNANCE Mark Bevir

THE GREAT DEPRESSION AND THE
    NEW DEAL Eric Rauchway
HABERMAS James Gordon Finlayson
HAPPINESS Daniel M. Haybron
HEGEL Peter Singer
HEIDEGGER Michael Inwood
HERODOTUS Jennifer T. Roberts
HIEROGLYPHS Penelope Wilson
HINDUISM Kim Knott
HISTORY John H. Arnold
THE HISTORY OF ASTRONOMY
    Michael Hoskin
THE HISTORY OF LIFE Michael Benton
THE HISTORY OF MATHEMATICS
    Jacqueline Stedall
THE HISTORY OF MEDICINE
    William Bynum
THE HISTORY OF TIME
    Leofranc Holford-Strevens
HIV/AIDS Alan Whiteside
HOBBES Richard Tuck
HORMONES Martin Luck
HUMAN EVOLUTION Bernard Wood
HUMAN RIGHTS Andrew Clapham
HUMANISM Stephen Law
HUME A. J. Ayer
HUMOUR Noël Carroll
THE ICE AGE Jamie Woodward
IDEOLOGY Michael Freeden
INDIAN PHILOSOPHY Sue Hamilton
INFORMATION Luciano Floridi
INNOVATION Mark Dodgson and
    David Gann
INTELLIGENCE Ian J. Deary
INTERNATIONAL MIGRATION
    Khalid Koser
INTERNATIONAL RELATIONS
    Paul Wilkinson
INTERNATIONAL SECURITY
    Christopher S. Browning
IRAN Ali M. Ansari
ISLAM Malise Ruthven
ISLAMIC HISTORY Adam Silverstein
ITALIAN LITERATURE
    Peter Hainsworth and David Robey
JESUS Richard Bauckham
JOURNALISM Ian Hargreaves
JUDAISM Norman Solomon
JUNG Anthony Stevens
KABBALAH Joseph Dan

KAFKA Ritchie Robertson
KANT Roger Scruton
KEYNES Robert Skidelsky
KIERKEGAARD Patrick Gardiner
KNOWLEDGE Jennifer Nagel
THE KORAN Michael Cook
LANDSCAPE ARCHITECTURE
    Ian H. Thompson
LANDSCAPES AND
    GEOMORPHOLOGY
    Andrew Goudie and Heather Viles
LANGUAGES Stephen R. Anderson
LATE ANTIQUITY Gillian Clark
LAW Raymond Wacks
THE LAWS OF THERMODYNAMICS
    Peter Atkins
LEADERSHIP Keith Grint
LINCOLN Allen C. Guelzo
LINGUISTICS Peter Matthews
LITERARY THEORY Jonathan Culler
LOCKE John Dunn
LOGIC Graham Priest
MACHIAVELLI Quentin Skinner
MADNESS Andrew Scull
MAGIC Owen Davies
MAGNA CARTA Nicholas Vincent
MAGNETISM Stephen Blundell
MALTHUS Donald Winch
MANAGEMENT John Hendry
MAO Delia Davin
MARINE BIOLOGY Philip V. Mladenov
THE MARQUIS DE SADE John Phillips
MARTIN LUTHER Scott H. Hendrix
MARTYRDOM Jolyon Mitchell
MARX Peter Singer
MATERIALS Christopher Hall
MATHEMATICS Timothy Gowers
THE MEANING OF LIFE
    Terry Eagleton
MEDICAL ETHICS Tony Hope
MEDICAL LAW Charles Foster
MEDIEVAL BRITAIN John Gillingham
    and Ralph A. Griffiths
MEMORY Jonathan K. Foster
METAPHYSICS Stephen Mumford
MICHAEL FARADAY Frank A. J. L. James
MICROECONOMICS Avinash Dixit
THE MIDDLE AGES Miri Rubin
MINERALS David Vaughan
MODERN ART David Cottington

MODERN CHINA Rana Mitter
MODERN FRANCE
    Vanessa R. Schwartz
MODERN IRELAND Senia Pašeta
MODERN JAPAN
    Christopher Goto-Jones
MODERN LATIN AMERICAN
    LITERATURE
    Roberto González Echevarría
MODERN WAR Richard English
MODERNISM Christopher Butler
MOLECULES Philip Ball
THE MONGOLS Morris Rossabi
MORMONISM Richard Lyman Bushman
MUHAMMAD Jonathan A. C. Brown
MULTICULTURALISM Ali Rattansi
MUSIC Nicholas Cook
MYTH Robert A. Segal
THE NAPOLEONIC WARS
    Mike Rapport
NATIONALISM Steven Grosby
NELSON MANDELA Elleke Boehmer
NEOLIBERALISM Manfred Steger and
    Ravi Roy
NETWORKS Guido Caldarelli and
    Michele Catanzaro
THE NEW TESTAMENT
    Luke Timothy Johnson
THE NEW TESTAMENT AS
    LITERATURE Kyle Keefer
NEWTON Robert Iliffe
NIETZSCHE Michael Tanner
NINETEENTH-CENTURY BRITAIN
    Christopher Harvie and H. C. G. Matthew
THE NORMAN CONQUEST
    George Garnett
NORTH AMERICAN
    INDIANS Theda Perdue and
    Michael D. Green
NORTHERN IRELAND
    Marc Mulholland
NOTHING Frank Close
NUCLEAR POWER Maxwell Irvine
NUCLEAR WEAPONS
    Joseph M. Siracusa
NUMBERS Peter M. Higgins
NUTRITION David A. Bender
OBJECTIVITY Stephen Gaukroger
THE OLD TESTAMENT
    Michael D. Coogan

THE ORCHESTRA D. Kern Holoman
ORGANIZATIONS Mary Jo Hatch
PAGANISM Owen Davies
THE PALESTINIAN-ISRAELI
    CONFLICT Martin Bunton
PARTICLE PHYSICS Frank Close
PAUL E. P. Sanders
PEACE Oliver P. Richmond
PENTECOSTALISM William K. Kay
THE PERIODIC TABLE Eric R. Scerri
PHILOSOPHY Edward Craig
PHILOSOPHY OF LAW Raymond Wacks
PHILOSOPHY OF SCIENCE
    Samir Okasha
PHOTOGRAPHY Steve Edwards
PHYSICAL CHEMISTRY Peter Atkins
PLAGUE Paul Slack
PLANETS David A. Rothery
PLANTS Timothy Walker
PLATO Julia Annas
POLITICAL PHILOSOPHY David Miller
POLITICS Kenneth Minogue
POSTCOLONIALISM Robert Young
POSTMODERNISM Christopher Butler
POSTSTRUCTURALISM Catherine Belsey
PREHISTORY Chris Gosden
PRESOCRATIC PHILOSOPHY
    Catherine Osborne
PRIVACY Raymond Wacks
PROBABILITY John Haigh
PROGRESSIVISM Walter Nugent
PROTESTANTISM Mark A. Noll
PSYCHIATRY Tom Burns
PSYCHOLOGY Gillian Butler and
    Freda McManus
PURITANISM Francis J. Bremer
THE QUAKERS Pink Dandelion
QUANTUM THEORY
    John Polkinghorne
RACISM Ali Rattansi
RADIOACTIVITY Claudio Tuniz
RASTAFARI Ennis B. Edmonds
THE REAGAN REVOLUTION Gil Troy
REALITY Jan Westerhoff
THE REFORMATION Peter Marshall
RELATIVITY Russell Stannard
RELIGION IN AMERICA Timothy Beal
THE RENAISSANCE Jerry Brotton
RENAISSANCE ART Geraldine A. Johnson
REVOLUTIONS Jack A. Goldstone

RHETORIC Richard Toye
RISK Baruch Fischhoff and John Kadvany
RIVERS Nick Middleton
ROBOTICS Alan Winfield
ROMAN BRITAIN Peter Salway
THE ROMAN EMPIRE
    Christopher Kelly
THE ROMAN REPUBLIC
    David M. Gwynn
ROMANTICISM Michael Ferber
ROUSSEAU Robert Wokler
RUSSELL A. C. Grayling
RUSSIAN HISTORY Geoffrey Hosking
RUSSIAN LITERATURE Catriona Kelly
THE RUSSIAN REVOLUTION
    S. A. Smith
SCHIZOPHRENIA Chris Frith and
    Eve Johnstone
SCHOPENHAUER Christopher Janaway
SCIENCE AND RELIGION
    Thomas Dixon
SCIENCE FICTION David Seed
THE SCIENTIFIC REVOLUTION
    Lawrence M. Principe
SCOTLAND Rab Houston
SEXUALITY Véronique Mottier
SHAKESPEARE Germaine Greer
SIKHISM Eleanor Nesbitt
THE SILK ROAD James A. Millward
SLEEP Steven W. Lockley and
    Russell G. Foster
SOCIAL AND CULTURAL
    ANTHROPOLOGY
    John Monaghan and Peter Just
SOCIALISM Michael Newman
SOCIOLINGUISTICS John Edwards
SOCIOLOGY Steve Bruce
SOCRATES C. C. W. Taylor
THE SOVIET UNION Stephen Lovell
THE SPANISH CIVIL WAR
    Helen Graham
SPANISH LITERATURE Jo Labanyi
SPINOZA Roger Scruton
SPIRITUALITY Philip Sheldrake
STARS Andrew King
STATISTICS David J. Hand
STEM CELLS Jonathan Slack
STRUCTURAL ENGINEERING
    David Blockley
STUART BRITAIN John Morrill

SUPERCONDUCTIVITY
    Stephen Blundell
SYMMETRY Ian Stewart
TEETH Peter S. Ungar
TERRORISM Charles Townshend
THEOLOGY David F. Ford
THOMAS AQUINAS Fergus Kerr
THOUGHT Tim Bayne
TIBETAN BUDDHISM
    Matthew T. Kapstein
TOCQUEVILLE Harvey C. Mansfield
TRAGEDY Adrian Poole
THEATRE Marvin Carlson
THE TROJAN WAR Eric H. Cline
TRUST Katherine Hawley
THE TUDORS John Guy
TWENTIETH-CENTURY BRITAIN
    Kenneth O. Morgan

THE UNITED NATIONS
    Jussi M. Hanhimäki
THE U.S. CONGRESS
    Donald A. Ritchie
THE U.S. SUPREME COURT
    Linda Greenhouse
UTOPIANISM Lyman Tower Sargent
THE VIKINGS Julian Richards
VIRUSES Dorothy H. Crawford
WITCHCRAFT Malcolm Gaskill
WITTGENSTEIN A. C. Grayling
WORK Stephen Fineman
WORLD MUSIC Philip Bohlman
THE WORLD TRADE
    ORGANIZATION Amrita Narlikar
WORLD WAR II Gerhard L. Weinberg
WRITING AND SCRIPT
    Andrew Robinson

Available soon:

CHILD PSYCHOLOGY Usha Goswami
SPORT Mike Cronin
MICROBIOLOGY
    Nicholas P. Money

CORPORATE SOCIAL
    RESPONSIBILITY Jeremy Moon
PSYCHOTHERAPY Tom Burns and
    Eva Burns-Lundgren

For more information visit our website

www.oup.com/vsi/

Gerhard L. Weinberg

WORLD WAR II

A Very Short Introduction

OXFORD
UNIVERSITY PRESS

OXFORD
UNIVERSITY PRESS

Great Clarendon Street, Oxford, OX2 6DP,
United Kingdom

Oxford University Press is a department of the University of Oxford.
It furthers the University's objective of excellence in research, scholarship,
and education by publishing worldwide. Oxford is a registered trade mark of
Oxford University Press in the UK and in certain other countries

© Gerhard L. Weinberg 2014

The moral rights of the author have been asserted

First edition published in 2014

Impression: 12

Published in the United States of America by Oxford University Press
198 Madison Avenue, New York, NY 10016, United States of America

British Library Cataloguing in Publication Data

Data available

Library of Congress Control Number: 2014942238

ISBN 978-0-19-968877-7

Printed in Great Britain by
Ashford Colour Press Ltd., Gosport, Hampshire.

Contents

List of maps xiii

Introduction 1

1 The inter-war years 4

2 World War II begins 20

3 War in the West: 1940 33

4 Barbarossa: the German invasion of the Soviet Union 52

5 Japan expands its war with China 66

6 The turning tide: autumn 1942–spring 1944 81

7 Developments on the home front and in technical and medical fields 98

8 Allied victory, 1944–5 110

Conclusion 123

Further reading 127

Index 131

List of maps

1   Polish campaign **21**

2   Norwegian campaign **29**

3   Fall of France **36-7**

4   a. The campaign against
    Yugoslavia **48**

    b. Balkan campaign **49**

5   Barbarossa **56**

6   German–Soviet Front,
    1941 **62**

7   The Philippines 1941–42 **74**

8   The East Indies 1941–42 **75**

9   German-Soviet War
    1942–43 **83**

10 Battle of Kursk **85**

11 Sicilian campaign **92**

12 Overlord **113**

13 German–Soviet War
    1943–44 **115**

14 Philippines campaign
    1944 45 **118**

15 The Okinawa campaign
    1945 **120**

Introduction

For decades, 11 November was remembered as the day on which
the fighting stopped in 1918 in what was long called 'The Great
War' before many started to refer to it as World War I. Both
the memorializing of the end of the conflict that raged around the
world from 1914 to 1918 and the name it was given reflect the
unprecedented enormity of the casualties and destruction incurred
in that conflict. There had been exceedingly bloody wars before
1914, and some had included fighting on lands and oceans around
the globe, but none had drawn in so many countries and colonial
territories, involved directly or indirectly so large a proportion of
the people on earth at the time, and ended the lives of such vast
numbers even as it uprooted empires and dynasties. If at its end
there was such great relief and a widespread hope that nothing like
this would ever happen again, we must wonder how it was that a
mere 20 years after 1918 there was a near repetition and then, one
year later, a second, worldwide, conflagration did begin.

Some who look back on World War II insist that one should consider
it to have begun in 1931 with the Japanese seizure of Manchuria, or
in 1935 with the Italian invasion of Abyssinia/Ethiopia, or in 1936
with the outbreak of the Spanish Civil War, or in 1937 with the start
of open hostilities between Japan and China. The view taken here is
that these conflicts were of a different sort. Both of the dates from
east Asia marked a resumption of local expansionist drives by Japan;

the Italian operation in northeast Africa was a resumption of Italy's colonial expansion; and the Spanish Civil War began and remained a conflict within that one country. Although in all these cases other powers provided aid to one side or another, there was no open participation of countries other than those immediately engaged. It is true that Japan, in December 1941, deliberately joined the wider conflict that Germany had initiated in 1939, but this choice, to be examined in Chapter 5, was in no way foreordained. Since 1945, there have been wars between individual countries and civil wars within countries, but there has—most fortunately—been no instance of worldwide military hostilities.

If for the purposes of this study the war reviewed began in 1939, why should it be considered a world war from the beginning rather than a European war that, like many of its predecessors, became a world war only in and after 1941? Although the war started in Europe, it had worldwide aspects and participants from the very beginning. Germany, which initiated the conflict, had ambitions that embraced the whole globe, as will be demonstrated in Chapter 1. The Allies included Canada, Australia, and New Zealand right away, with the Union of South Africa joining them a few days later. The French and British colonial empires were also involved from the very beginning as shown by the soldiers from French colonies in Africa who fought in France—and where thousands were shot by the Germans after surrendering—and by the raising of the war's largest volunteer army in India. Although Italy's participation did not begin until June 1940, it brought with it a more direct involvement of the African continent; and no one would suggest that the anti-British uprising in Iraq and the fighting in Syria in May and June of 1941 occurred anywhere but in Asia.

The war on the oceans was also worldwide from the beginning. Just two examples: the battle between the German pocket battleship *Graf Spee* and the British cruisers *Exeter*, *Ajax*, and *Achilles* off the coast of Uruguay in December 1939, and the assistance the Soviet Union provided to Germany, sending an auxiliary cruiser across the passage north of Siberia in 1940 so that it could sink Allied ships in the Pacific. Both the German submarine campaign and British efforts to intercept German merchant ships also occurred all over the globe.

If, therefore, World War II is considered as having begun in September 1939 with the German invasion of Poland and ended in September 1945 with the surrender of Japan, how did this come about? There has been almost endless argument over who was responsible for starting World War I, but very little about German responsibility for initiating World War II. A major issue that forms the focus of Chapter 1 is why and how this happened in a world where the memory of the prior terrible war was exceedingly vivid in the memory of all adults who had survived it. Since Germany started the war expecting to win it, and for a while appeared to have a reasonable chance of accomplishing that aim, how did it come to be that the Allies won? Subsequent chapters will examine that question. They will do so in a manner that includes both those who became involved on Germany's side and those who found themselves on the side of Britain and France, whether when attacked, like the Soviet Union and the United States, or through joining willingly like Italy, Japan, Hungary, Finland, Romania, Bulgaria, on one side, and most countries of the western hemisphere on the other.

Because the war developed into the greatest such conflict in history, it will also be necessary to engage the changes the war produced within the belligerents and the empires that some of them had had before they became involved. Something will also need to be included about the dramatic changes in weapons on the one hand and medicine and technology on the other hand. The computer on which the text of this book is drafted, for example, may serve as an illustration of the way new mechanics developed and applied during the war now affect the daily lives of people in the present and into the future.

Chapter 1
The inter-war years

The 1919 peace conference

The representatives of the victorious powers who drafted the peace
treaties with Germany, Austria, Hungary, Bulgaria, and the successor
of the Ottoman Empire faced numerous complicated problems. How
to treat the defeated Central Powers; how to deal with new states
emerging from the ruins of the Russian, Austro-Hungarian, and
Ottoman empires; how to handle the conflict between China and
Japan over the former German colony in China; what to do about the
other German colonies; and how to reduce the danger of a disaster
like the one just ended from occurring again. Although rarely
mentioned in the literature on the Paris peace conference of 1919, it is
helpful to see many of these puzzles as facets of a fundamental issue:
how to reorganize Europe and territories elsewhere as the basic
assumption of territoriality shifted from the dynastic to the national
principle. That problem had not bothered the peacemakers of 1815
after the upheavals of the French Revolution and Napoleonic Wars.
In the thinking of many in Paris, it was the failure to adjust to the
national principle, obvious in the Balkan Wars of the early 20th
century and the struggle between Serbia and Austria-Hungary, that
was largely responsible for the conflict which had just ended.

The efforts of the peacemakers to engage with this fundamental
issue—how to facilitate a shift from states based on allegiance to a

dynasty to states based on the national identity of their people—were not entirely fair or reasonable, but they have rarely received the credit they merit. The number of people who believed themselves under rulers alien to themselves had been greatly reduced in Europe. Furthermore, there were three aspects of the peace settlement as a whole that fitted into this effort at adjustment and should be so seen. Several of the new states in Europe were obliged to sign treaties promising to respect the rights of national minorities living within their newly redrawn national boundaries. This system for the protection of national minorities did not function as well as its creators had hoped, but they do deserve credit for their efforts. The second feature of the peace settlement that fits into this concept of adjusting boundaries to nationality was the provision for plebiscites in several areas in Europe in which the inhabitants would vote on what nationality they considered themselves to be, with the intention that the boundaries drawn thereafter should reflect their expressed preferences. Here too problems would arise, but once again the idea deserves credit.

The third aspect of the peace settlement that focused on this new direction of the ruled rather than the rulers could be seen in the arrangement for the German colonial empire and the non-Turkish portions of the Ottoman Empire. Very small parts of German colonies, Cameroon and Togo in west Africa, were incorporated into adjacent British and French colonies, and a tiny piece of German East Africa (Tanzania) was added to the Portuguese colony of Mozambique, but the bulk of Germany's colonial empire was turned into what were called 'Mandates', as were the parts of the Ottoman Empire allocated to Britain and France. The mandates were classified into three categories: the As could expect to become independent states fairly soon; the Bs could expect this process to take longer; and the Cs could expect to be under outside control for a long time. These countries were allocated to different victor countries until they could attain independence, and their new rulers were expected to report on them to a special committee of the newly established international organization. There is a significant

5

difference between this procedure and that after prior worldwide conflicts when territories like parts of India, Canada, and other portions of the Western hemisphere, Asia, and Pacific islands were transferred from one colonial empire to another without regard for the possibility that the inhabitants might prefer at some time to be ruled from their own capital rather than from London, Paris, Madrid, Lisbon, Washington, Tokyo, Rome, or elsewhere.

Two additional innovations must be mentioned. With considerable American influence, a new international organization called The League of Nations was created. Its charter, called the Covenant, was included as the first part in each peace treaty. The idea was that the terrible war just past should make a new approach to international relations necessary in the hope of preventing any further repetition. There would be a permanent international forum for the discussion of whatever issues were pressing at the time; a mechanism for watching over minorities, mandates, and plebiscites; and a collective form of protection for the independence of each member of the organization. It would not work out as well as hoped for, but the concept introduced a new element into international relations that played a part in the thinking of people and leaders for the rest of the century.

The other innovation was the inclusion in the peace treaty with Germany of a provision for trials of war criminals. This was one of the provisions most hated by the Germans, and eventually there were no international trials; instead responsibility shifted to a German court meeting in Leipzig. Those trials proved to be a farce that led to a different approach during and after World War II, but again the concept brought a new element into the way people came to think about the horrors of war. It was not surprising that the captain of a submarine who had torpedoed a hospital ship and then ordered the machine-gunning of lifeboats with survivors could expect a great career in Germany after the National Socialists came to power there, but the treaty demonstrated a new way of considering such activities.

Since both Austria-Hungary and the Ottoman Empire disappeared at the end of the conflict, it was the peace treaty with Germany that was of the greatest importance. It was in it that the shift from the dynastic to the national principle proved both most important and most controversial. Although it was the newest of the great powers, having existed for less than half a century, Germany was not broken up. The people living there clearly thought of themselves as Germans more than as Prussians, Würtembergers, Saxons, or Bavarians. On the one hand, territory taken from others in the preceding century and a half would be returned to prior owners: France, Denmark, and Poland; but no substantial portion of territory clearly inhabited by Germans was turned over to the victors. These decisions of the peacemakers raised serious questions for the future.

In connection with the return of lands to Denmark and Poland, plebiscites were to be held in areas where there was doubt as to where the new boundary should be placed, and this was also provided for the Saar territory that would go on to be separated from Germany for 15 years. The return of land taken from Poland aroused the most violent objections in Germany. In the three partitions of Poland in 1772, 1793, and 1795, the rulers of Brandenburg-Prussia had seized large areas from that country in a process that brought Russia closer to central Europe and, in the first, created an east–west corridor connecting Brandenburg and Prussia. The return to Poland of much of the land taken from it, which, as pre-1772, meant a corridor running north–south, was considered an outrage by many Germans even though Poland had existed as a state many times longer than had Germany. One facet of this outrage was of enormous importance then as it has been in subsequent decades. Very many Germans thought of the Poles and other Slavic peoples of Eastern Europe as racially and culturally inferior. The concept of asking people to vote whether they were Germans or Poles implied an equivalence considered insulting to many Germans, who thought of themselves as an entirely different category of human beings. When the German delegation at the peace conference persuaded the victors to substitute a plebiscite in Upper Silesia for its transfer to Poland as originally intended, with the implication that it might be divided as it eventually was, this was seen by many Germans not as a major success for its negotiating team but rather as another insult to their self-perception. The fact that many of the German states including Prussia, Bavaria, and Oldenburg had been and continued to be non-contiguous until 1945 was invariably overlooked.

Another aspect of great importance was the argument over Germany's western border and the way the peace conference resolved it. Since France had been invaded twice by the Germans in the recent past—in 1870 and in 1914—the French were concerned about possible future German aggression, in much the same way that many had worried about future French aggression in Europe in 1815. The option of detaching the Rhineland from Germany and creating a separate state there was considered seriously, but while this could protect France from invasion by Germany, it would involve a drastic violation of the national principle. At the insistence of the British and American delegations, the Rhineland was to remain with Germany under arrangements designed as an alternative protection for France and Belgium. The land west of the Rhine and the zone 50 kilometres east of it were to be and remain demilitarized. Furthermore, Britain and the United States signed treaties of guarantee with France that guaranteed they would come to the assistance of France if Germany did invade again. It was believed that these arrangements would provide security for France while upholding the national principle. Germany would retain the area but be discouraged from attacking France as that would mean automatically being at war with Britain and the United States. Germany would also be obliged to respect the independence of Poland and the small states that had arisen out of the Austro-Hungarian Empire since its own door to invasion from the west would be locked open by the demilitarized zone. However, the refusal of the United States' Senate to ratify the treaty of guarantee followed by Britain's refusal to be sole guarantor contributed to the collapse of the structure of peace in the 1930s. With the United States removing itself from the treaty system it had helped design, enforcement was left to the countries that had been most weakened by the war—and this encouraged the defeated to try again.

The treaty with Germany had two further categories of provisions the Germans greatly resented and found ways to undermine or disregard. These were limitations on Germany's military and provision for reparations. The Germans had introduced into warfare the bombing of cities far removed from the front, and the Allies, not sharing their enthusiasm for this approach, prohibited Germany from having a military air force. Nonetheless, the Germans learned in World War II that others would reciprocate if they insisted on bombing cities, but after 1918 they utilized facilities provided by their Soviet friends to evade this restriction. They did the same thing when barred from developing armoured vehicles, and turned to other venues to circumvent the prohibition on submarines. As for the treaty's limitation on the size of their army to 100,000, this was evaded by, for example, training up militarized police. While the treaty had been made law by the German parliament, the highest German military commanders, despite having sworn an oath on the constitution and the laws of the republic, took great pride in breaking that oath as frequently as possible.

After previous wars, the victors had frequently imposed an indemnity on the loser, a recent example being the indemnity the new Germany imposed on France in 1871. Those drawing up the peace treaty put this differently. The bulk of the fighting and attendant destruction had taken place outside Germany, so the term 'reparations' utilized in the treaty and subsequent negotiations and debates was to show that instead of being fined for losing, Germany was to pay the costs of repairing the damage it had caused. The long and complicated story about reparations cannot be reviewed here, but the key outcomes must be mentioned since they affected subsequent events inside both Germany and the victor countries. To avoid paying reparations, the German government in 1923 deliberately destroyed the value of its currency through inflation and in 1931–2 turned to drastic deflation. The result internationally was that Germany paid very little and the victors had to pay their own repair costs, leading to them being further weakened as a result. The effect in Germany, however, was a tremendous dissatisfaction domestically with the government and greater willingness to support the different type of regime the National Socialists advocated.

Germany after World War I and the rise of Hitler

In the confused situation inside Germany after a defeat that practically no one had anticipated, various groups and individuals came forward with explanations for what had happened and proposals for a different future. Many of the military and some of the political leaders argued that Germany had not been defeated at the front but had been stabbed in the back by socialists, communists, Jews, and other allegedly subversive elements. As beneficiaries of the defeat they had caused, these now ruled the state. A new system in which there would be no room for domestic differences illustrated by multiple political parties would guarantee victory in future wars for a state led by one leader of the only political party. It was the National Socialist Party led by Adolf Hitler that drew increasing support with such a message. In the erroneous belief that they could control this movement and in the expectation of a different outcome in any future war, the men around the elected president of Germany, Paul von Hindenburg, persuaded him to appoint Hitler as chancellor at the end of January 1933.

In his writings and speeches Hitler had held to the stab-in-the-back legend and had praised the Soviet and Italian fascist systems for allowing only one political party. He had insisted that the road to Germany's future lay NOT in wars to regain the snippets of land lost in the peace treaty—the stupidity advocated by what he called 'Grenzpolitiker', border politicians—but in wars to gain enormous 'Lebensraum', living space, as demanded by a 'Raumpolitiker', a politician of space, like himself. In a few months during 1933, Hitler consolidated a one-party dictatorship in Germany, and simultaneously accelerated the rearmament that had been going on secretly. He explained to the military commanders a few days after becoming chancellor that this was for the conquest and Germanization of vast living space in Eastern Europe.

Hitler assumed that substantial acceleration of the previously secret rearmament would suffice for the first of the wars he intended, that being against Czechoslovakia, with which he planned to consolidate Germany's position in central Europe and increase the army divisions it could raise. New weapons, especially single-engine and two-engine dive bombers, larger tanks, and major warships, would be needed for the next war. And this war would be against France and Britain, the countries that had caused Germany great difficulties in the last conflict. While the defeat of the Western powers was seen as a necessary prerequisite, Hitler's assumption was that in the planned subsequent invasion of the Soviet Union, no new weapons would be needed. His view was that there would be no difficulty in defeating this country of inferior Slavic peoples, who, by what Hitler considered a stroke of good fortune for Germany, had been deprived of their prior, largely Germanic, ruling elite by the Bolshevik revolution and were now governed by, in Hitler's view, incompetents. The crushing of the inferior Soviets would provide the raw materials, especially oil, needed for the subsequent war against the United States. That country, though also racially inferior, was far away and had a substantial navy. In 1937, therefore, as soon as design and production of the weapons for war against France and Britain were well under way, Hitler ordered the initiation of plans for and construction of the intercontinental bombers and super-battleships required for war against the United States, since these, as he correctly anticipated, would take years to design and build.

The world reacts to Hitler

The countries of the world other than Germany were not prepared to believe that, after the experience of what was then called the Great War, anyone would seriously intend to start new wars likely to involve most of the world. There were all sorts of efforts to limit armaments in the 1920s and early 1930s. While not very effective, these demonstrated what most major powers thought was needed; and Germany's formal withdrawal in 1933 was not taken as a sign of determination for renewed conflict. Similarly, the withdrawal of Japan from naval limitation agreements was answered by the United States, and to a lesser extent by Britain, merely with some minimal naval rearmament of their own. Japan's seizure of Manchuria in 1931 and renewed war with China in 1937 were regarded with disapproval but met no military response from other countries. It was Germany, because of its excellent relations with both China and Japan, that tried hard to mediate the conflict in the autumn and winter of 1937. When the Tokyo government rejected any accommodation with the Chinese Nationalist government, Hitler opted to support Japan. He had also long argued for an alliance with Italy, both because he admired its dictator Benito Mussolini and because it could expand its empire only at the expense of its Great War allies. The same was true of Japan, which made it another opportune candidate for an alliance.

As Germany rearmed ever more openly in the 1930s, the United States' Congress enacted what were called 'neutrality laws'. These laws might have kept the United States out of the 1914 war, but now made another war more likely, being both a discouraging move for France and Britain and an encouraging one for Germany. Neither the French nor the British government was willing to go to war to halt Germany's open violations of the peace treaty. After the enormous casualties of the Great War, the public in both countries contemplated any renewed conflict with reluctance and horror. Britain had disarmed very extensively, and the French had initiated the construction of a major line of fortifications in the hope of discouraging or, alternatively, warding off, any renewed German invasion. People and leaders in both countries were also affected by the endless German complaints about the allegedly excessively harsh 1919 peace treaty. One of the German generals captured in Tunisia in May 1943 was taped commenting to other captured generals in February 1944 that they would all jump to the ceiling for joy if Germany could secure another Treaty of Versailles. However, that recognition came too late for the Germans who had succeeded in persuading many in the victorious countries to allow Germany great latitude in disregarding that treaty's terms.

With Germany becoming increasingly aligned with Italy and Japan, Britain felt further discouraged from confronting Germany. The threats to the British Empire and Commonwealth around the globe made for caution in Europe as well as the Mediterranean and east Asia. Bitter internal divisions weakened the position of France at the same time as it knew itself deprived of the support from the United States and Britain which it had been promised in exchange for leaving the Rhineland within Germany. When the Germans broke the other part of that arrangement in March 1936 by remilitarizing the Rhineland, the French government decided they would still not respond with military action. Treaties that France had signed with several of the new East European states were not seen as effective substitutes for the Franco-Russian alliance of the pre-1914 era, and a treaty with the Soviet Union agreed to in 1935 did not look helpful when the Soviet leader, Josef Stalin, was decapitating that country's army by a massive purge and there was no common border between Germany and the Soviet Union.

When, in March 1938, Hitler ordered the German army to march into Austria, no country was willing to fight for the independence of a people who, as the pictures and reports showed, were delighted to lose it. It would take the Austrians seven years of being German to discover that they were not German after all. However, the annexing of Austria had several significant immediate effects. Hitler's support within Germany received another boost; Germany acquired substantial economic assets as well as new borders directly with Italy, Hungary, and Yugoslavia; and Germany greatly increased its threat to Czechoslovakia.

The crisis over Czechoslovakia

Hitler expected to invade Czechoslovakia in the autumn of 1938 and to take over almost the whole country, possibly leaving its easternmost province to Hungary and a tiny bit to Poland. This, the first of his planned wars, was to be isolated from outside intervention by geography and propaganda. The geographic aspect was clear from a map of Europe: with the exception of a short border with Romania, the countries bordering Czechoslovakia were all its enemies, with territorial demands on it. The propaganda aspect was the presence inside Czechoslovakia of some three million Germans, primarily living in the border regions of the Bohemian portion of the country. If sufficient attention were focused on the pretended sufferings of this minority, and its members encouraged to create enough violent incidents, the German invasion of Czechoslovakia could be perceived as a deserved punishment with which others would not interfere. After all, boundaries had been drawn to follow the preferences of the various populations; the fact that, in the process, the state of Czechoslovakia would disappear would occur, in Hitler's view, too late for anyone to prevent it.

The German propaganda campaign worked very well, though in the end it had an unanticipated effect. The British government urged the leaders of Czechoslovakia to make extensive concessions to the German minority at the same time as Hitler told them to keep raising their demands. In July 1938, the French government secretly told the Czech government that France could not and would not fight over the issue of the German minority; and the dominions of Canada, the Union of South Africa, and Australia gave London similar warnings. The British prime minister, Neville Chamberlain, still hoped that war could be avoided by offering concessions on the part of the Czech government; and while Winston Churchill publicly criticized this approach, he confidentially advised the Prague authorities that, if he had been in power, he would have followed the same policy.

When it looked as if Germany was about to strike, Chamberlain insisted on flying to Germany. Hitler, who still intended to go to war, could not refuse to receive the British prime minister. Expecting that this demand would not be met, he insisted that Czechoslovakia yield its border areas with both the German minority and its defensive fortifications. To Hitler's surprise and disappointment, Chamberlain obtained the agreement of the Prague government and conveyed it to him in a second meeting. When Hitler then raised additional demands to avoid a peaceful settlement, both the British and French governments recognized that Germany was looking for an excuse for war, initiated mobilization, and made clear that they would fight if Germany struck. In this context, and on learning that the German public still preferred peace, Hitler responded to an appeal from Mussolini—whose country was in no condition for a major conflict, after a war to conquer Abyssinia/Ethiopia and still being involved in aiding the Nationalist armies of Francisco Franco in the Spanish Civil War. Hitler cancelled the invasion of Czechoslovakia and agreed to a third meeting at Munich, where he settled for his ostensible rather than his real aim.

Germany starts World War II

The Munich agreement, according to which the border area of Bohemia with its predominantly German population was ceded to Germany, has generally been seen as a surrender to German aggression. While it not only led to a worldwide sigh of relief that a general war had been avoided, it was strongly resented by Hitler, who came to see it as the worst mistake of his career. Correctly or incorrectly, he believed that war at that time would have been better for Germany; consequently he not only decided that war would come in the following year, 1939, but that he would conduct it in such a way as to avoid being cheated out of it—which is what he thought Chamberlain had done in 1938. The remainder of Czechoslovakia would be taken at the first opportunity that Germany would help create; the German public was to be whipped up to war fever; and the war against the Western powers that he believed a prerequisite for the subsequent invasion of the Soviet Union would follow. To make it safe for Germany to concentrate its forces in the West, the country's Eastern neighbours had to be subordinated to Germany. In the winter of 1938–9, this subordination was obtained from Hungary and Lithuania, but not in the case of Poland.

The leaders of the revived Poland were willing to make concessions to Germany in serious negotiations. They were prepared to ease transit between the main German territory and East Prussia, and to partition the Free City of Danzig in a manner that would allocate the city itself to Germany, but they would not subordinate the whole country to Germany. Although aware of the country's weak position between a hostile Germany and an equally hostile Soviet Union, they were determined to fight rather than abdicate their independence. This position of Poland coincided with a shift in the policies of France and Britain.

The obvious dissatisfaction of Germany with the annexation of the Czech borderlands, which was supposed to have been Germany's last demand, led to new perspectives in Paris and London. Rumours in the winter about a possible German strike on the Low Countries, Romania, and Poland brought a shift in which both governments came to the conclusion that if Germany attacked any country that chose to defend itself, whether in Western or Eastern Europe, they would come to its assistance. This view was reinforced by Germany's subsequent occupation of the major and central area of Czechoslovakia in March 1939, which showed that it had never been the German minority inside Czechoslovakia that concerned the Berlin government. This step hardened the willingness of the two Western powers to prepare to fight at Germany's next aggression, if the victim defended itself. With this resolution made, Britain introduced its first ever peacetime conscription policy. After the Second World War, it meant agreement by the Allies to the forced transfer of the German minority into Germany. They had cried 'Heim ins Reich', Home into the Reich; they would get their wish in a manner they had not anticipated.

Hitler hoped for an isolated campaign against Poland, which was seen as a necessary preliminary to an attack on France and Britain; however, he was prepared to face all three simultaneously. Since he scheduled the invasion of Poland for the autumn, he expected that winter would delay any serious retaliation from the West. Furthermore, a public alliance with Italy and negotiations with Japan were seen as ways to discourage Britain and France from intervening. However, fighting with the Red Army on the border between the puppet state of Manchukuo and the Soviet client state of Mongolia—the Nomonhan or Khalkin-Gol incident—made the Japanese unwilling to commit themselves at that time. An obvious alternative to agreement with Japan from the perspective of Berlin was agreement with the Soviet Union, which wanted major territorial gains from Poland and could assist Germany in bypassing any blockade when at war with the Western powers.

Relations between Germany and the Soviet Union had been good before Hitler came to power, and Stalin had repeatedly tried to restore them thereafter, but until the winter of 1938–9 Hitler had rebuffed such efforts since the Soviet Union had no common border with Austria or Czechoslovakia. However, the situation was different now. Just as Hitler believed in the racial inferiority of the Slavic people whom he thought Germany could easily crush at the appropriate time, so Stalin believed that fascism was a stage of capitalism, that it was in the Soviet interest for the capitalist states to fight each other, and that the agrarian expansionist doctrines of the Nazis were merely a cover for the real aims of a regime subservient to money interests seeking markets and profits. Disregarding the warning of American president Franklin Roosevelt that a Germany victorious in Western Europe would then turn against the Soviet Union and the United States, Stalin utilized publicly announced alliance negotiations with Britain and France to advance secret negotiations with Germany. Since Hitler expected to take over everything yielded to the Soviet Union and even more once France and Britain had been crushed, he was prepared to offer whatever Stalin wanted. When German foreign minister Joachim von Ribbentrop was sent to Moscow in August 1939 to sign a non-aggression pact and a secret protocol dividing Eastern Europe as discussed in diplomatic contacts, he was authorized to give away even more than Stalin asked for. An economic treaty preceded the agreements signed in Moscow on 23 August and assured Germany of a means to break any blockade as well as a partner in the destruction of Poland.

When Hitler learned that agreement had been reached in Moscow, the invasion of Poland was ordered. Warned by Chamberlain that Britain would stand by its commitment to Poland, he postponed the invasion for a few days in a further effort to discourage London, but then he ordered the attack. This time he had made sure that Germany could not be trapped in any peace talks, as he believed had happened in 1938. Equally, there were no detailed negotiations with Poland, as there had been with Czechoslovakia, and the final supposedly moderate demands on Poland were announced to ensure the backing of the German home front but even these were kept secret until they could be declared lapsed. The German ambassadors in Warsaw, London, and Paris were kept from their posts in the last critical days by a German leader whose only fear, as he told his military commanders, was that at the last moment some 'Saukerl' (utter wretch) might propose a compromise.

Hitler's worry was unnecessary. The British government, which had just signed a formal alliance with Poland, delivered an ultimatum for Germany to withdraw its invading troops and declared war when, as expected, there was no withdrawal. France followed a similar procedure a few hours later. Canada, Australia, and New Zealand declared war on Germany, as, after a short interval, did the Union of South Africa. The colonial government of India declared war while Ireland announced neutrality. The French colonial empire was automatically involved in the conflict, and although Mussolini was not yet ready to join on Germany's side, a new worldwide war was clearly under way.

Chapter 2
World War II begins

The invasions of Poland

As soon as he realized that he could not separate the Western powers from Poland, Hitler ordered war to begin although his timetable had allowed one more day for negotiations. No formal declaration of war was issued. Early in the morning of 1 September 1939, German bombers made a terror attack on the Polish town of Wielun, levelling the community hospital, machine-gunning residents, and killing some 1,200 civilians. Similar attacks on other Polish towns soon followed as the Germans responded to President Roosevelt's plea to spare civilian targets by dropping a bomb on the grounds of the American embassy in Warsaw.

Due to the arguments in preceding years about responsibility for war in 1914, with much attention to the sequence of mobilizations, the Polish government had held back on mobilizing. Its plan for defending large parts of the country against invasion spread its forces too thinly to halt the German invaders at any of the places where they struck. Armoured columns assisted by tactical air support broke through rapidly at several points, and German infantry moved forward with or immediately behind the tanks. At some spots Polish units fought sufficiently well to slow the German advance, but such situations were soon negated by German columns by-passing the defenders (Map 1).

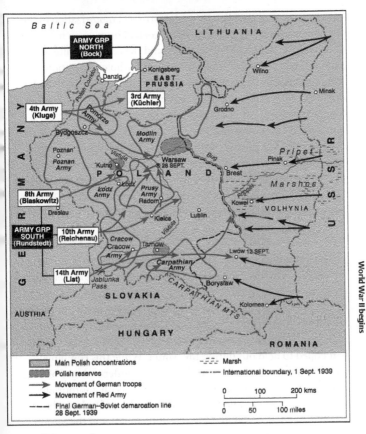

1. Polish campaign

Several aspects of the German drive into Poland must be noted.
While the employment of massed armour with support from the
German air force assisted the rapid breakthroughs and advances,
the wear on this equipment in the terrain and poor roads and
airfields was considerable, a point German military leaders failed
to take into account when preparing to invade the Soviet Union.
The heavy dependence of German forces on horses for all varieties
of transport from hauling artillery to moving the wounded was

obscured by propaganda movies that stressed motorization of the German army far beyond reality. Orders had been given before the attack for the killing of Polish clergy and the country's elite in general, since the expectation was that the whole population would eventually be replaced by German settlers so that potential organizers of resistance had to be removed as quickly as possible. Similarly, vast numbers of Polish civilians and substantial numbers of Jews were murdered as the German military began its descent into ever greater participation in what became genocide. In the campaign in Poland, there were distinct exceptions to this practice and serious objections from some in the German military. Such reluctance and objections drew the attention of the German leadership and produced new and additional approaches subsequently.

From the first days of war, the German government urged the Soviet Union to invade eastern Poland. At first Moscow held back, partly for political reasons and partly because of continued fighting with Japanese forces at Nomonhan. As soon as agreement to end hostilities was arranged with the defeated Japanese, the Red Army drove into eastern Poland, precisely where the Poles had hoped to hold out during the winter. While this combined with the German advance sealed the fate of independent Poland, it did not terminate Poland's role in the war. With appropriate ceremonies, German and Soviet troops moved to the boundary that had been included in the secret agreement; and the Soviets turned over to the Germans liberated German prisoners of war much more speedily and carefully than they would return liberated British and American prisoners of war in 1945. However, several Polish warships escaped to join the Allies, and numerous Polish soldiers also found their way out. Some Polish intelligence specialists made their way to the West, having just before the war provided the British and French with the critical information on their breaking into German enigma code machines.
A government-in-exile moved to London to represent Polish interests among the Allies, was officially recognized by the British

government, and was similarly recognized by the United States and many other countries.

A small British Expeditionary Force (BEF) joined the French forces being mobilized and moved into frontier fortifications; there was, however, no significant offensive move to relieve German pressure on Poland. What little air activity was mounted was strictly limited to attacks on military targets with German cities seeing only the dropping of leaflets. This began to change in 1940 after Germany's air force had carried its programme of terror attacks to cities in the West.

Germany formally annexed both the Free City of Danzig and a very substantial part of Poland. These annexed lands were to be Germanized by expelling large numbers of Poles, the majority of the inhabitants, and many Jews. The Poles were driven into the central portion of the former country now formed into a new unit called 'The General Government' which was subjected to harsh rule as it became the dumping ground for those expelled from their homes. By agreement with the Soviet Union, people of German cultural background from the Baltic States and later from parts of Romania annexed by the Soviets were moved into camps in German-controlled Poland. They were often settled in homes Poles had been expelled from, while others languished for years in camps. The point to be noted is that here, and in the simultaneous movement of many Germans out of the south Tyrol area turned over to Italy after the prior war, one can see the German alternative to the Allied principle of 1919. Instead of trying to adjust boundaries to the nationality of the inhabitants, the boundaries were to be drawn as suited the winner and then the inhabitants were to be adjusted to the new boundaries. While this procedure was applied to the Germans by the Allies at the end of the war, they did not adopt a further policy the Germans applied in parts of Eastern Europe that they conquered. Called the 'Heuaktion', Hay Operation, it involved the kidnapping of many thousands of babies and very young children who looked 'Germanic' and were turned over for adoption to German families.

War at sea

One sphere in which fighting between Germany and the Allies began in September 1939 and continued until the German surrender of May 1945 was on, under, and over the oceans. German warships and auxiliary warships (converted merchant ships) had in some cases been sent out into the world before the initiation of hostilities, and these now began raiding Allied merchant ships. Other warships were added in subsequent years. A dramatic event in this process was the battle between the German pocket battleship *Graf Spee* and three British cruisers off the coasts of Argentina and Uruguay in December 1939, in which the cruisers were damaged and the *Graf Spee* ended up being scuttled. German submarines began sinking ships on a substantial scale, with the sinking of the passenger ship *Athenia* on 3 September 1939 as a spectacular beginning. The British turned to a system of convoys more rapidly than in the prior conflict, but the 'Battle of the Atlantic' as it was called shifted back and forth thereafter. On the British side, the breaking into the German naval code at times proved helpful in routing ships and convoys around German submarine dispositions. These were frequently arranged in packs directed from and reporting to special headquarters on land by radio. When sighting a convoy, the leading submarine would summon the others in the pack for a combined attack. These radio messages were vulnerable to interception, but so were the British naval messages to and from the convoys. It might be best to generalize that into 1943 German decoding was at times ahead of the British, while thereafter the British, assisted by the Americans, were ahead of the Germans until the end of the war. The development of a short-range direction finder, referred to as 'Huff-Duff', also assisted the Allies in their campaign to defend shipping as did the increasing participation of the Canadian navy and, later, the provision of escort carriers by the United States.

Long-range airplanes, when assigned to this duty, played a significant role in the Allied effort as to a lesser extent did blimps.

Two other forms of assistance to the German campaign at sea must be mentioned. At times German long-range planes served as a means of finding ships and convoys that were difficult for submarines to locate. These planes also attacked ships, both the merchant ships and any escort vessels. The other form of aid came in the first years of war from the Soviet Union. Just as Stalin did not realize that helping the Germans drive the Allies off the continent first in the North, then in the West, and subsequently in the South would leave him alone with the Germans in the East, so he failed to see that Allied ships sunk with Soviet assistance could not rise from the sea floor to carry supplies to the Soviet Union after it was attacked by Germany. In the event, in exchange for some naval equipment and an uncompleted cruiser, he allowed the Germans to utilize the port of Murmansk for their naval activities, provided the German navy with a base on the Arctic Ocean west of Murmansk, and enabled a German auxiliary cruiser to transit the northern seaway across Siberia to enter the Pacific Ocean and sink Allied ships there. More important for the German war effort was the provision of large quantities of important supplies such as oil and non-ferrous metals and the trans-shipment of rubber and other critical materials from east Asia by train until the German invasion of the Soviet Union stopped the last trains.

While Soviet support for the German naval war probably contributed to the later objections of the commander-in-chief of the German Navy, Admiral Raeder, to a German attack on the Soviet Union, he did urge on Adolf Hitler two other moves in the naval war during the winter of 1939–40. Beginning in October 1939, he argued for the systematic sinking of American ships. Sharing the general assumption of German leaders that the role of the United States in the prior war had been of no importance, he was ready to resume hostilities with that country if it simplified the situation for German submarines by authorizing them to sink any ship they could find.

Hitler would not allow this at the time. Until Germany could either build its surface navy to deal with the United States or had an ally with such a navy, he preferred not to encourage the United States to mobilize its military potential. In the summer of 1940, the first step after the victory in the West would be his order for resumption of construction on the blue-water navy for war against the United States, but in the meantime he preferred to let the Americans sleep.

The German invasion of Denmark and Norway

The other move Admiral Raeder urged was a German occupation of Norway, with Denmark also seized to facilitate communications, so that Germany's navy would have better access to the Atlantic. The seizure of bases in Norway for war against Britain had been an interest of the German navy in World War I and continued to be high on its agenda in the inter-war years. Hitler similarly saw this as a major move in the war against Britain. A subsidiary advantage of occupying Norway would be that control of the waters off the Norwegian coast would assure safety for iron shipments from Sweden in the winter when much of the Baltic Sea was frozen but Germany depended on Swedish iron for 40 per cent of its needs. Hitler authorized preparations for such an operation and held to it when some in the naval high command expressed doubts. It was assumed from the beginning that Norway would become a permanent part of Germany with a major naval base at Trondheim, which was to become a German city with a super highway connecting it to the German mainland.

Hitler would very much have preferred to attack in the West through the three Low Countries in the late autumn of 1939. A combination of technical difficulties after the campaign in Poland, some objections from within the military, and primarily problems with the weather led to a series of postponements. In support of the German forces advancing against whatever resistance the invaded neutrals and the Allies might offer, the German air force was expected to provide extensive tactical support. It had, in fact, been designed primarily for such a role. Stretches of bad weather in the winter, therefore, played a significant role in causing postponements that led to the strike north preceding the German move in the West.

The fighting in the winter of 1939–40 that attracted most contemporary attention was that between the Soviet Union and Finland. Right after the joint German–Soviet defeat of Poland, the Soviet Union obliged the three Baltic States of Estonia, Latvia, and Lithuania to allow the stationing of Soviet forces in them. A simultaneous demand for territorial and other concessions from Finland led to negotiations which the Soviets ended by attacking that country on 30 November. Such a move had been considered in Moscow earlier, and a puppet government for what was assumed to become a quickly conquered country was established. The reality proved different from Soviet expectations. While in the northernmost portion of the front, the Red Army occupied the Finnish coast on the Arctic Ocean, both at the southern part and in the middle the Red Army encountered stubborn resistance and some local defeats. Massive reinforcement enabled the Soviets to drive back the Finns at the critical southern part of the front in February 1940. With some Swedish mediation, peace negotiations ended the fighting in March. Finland was obliged to cede territory to the Soviet Union in both the southern and central portions of the border and to allow a Soviet naval base in the southwest, but the Soviets evacuated the territory they had occupied in the north. The puppet government was dissolved and never installed in the territory seized from Finland. The Soviet Union was expelled from the League of Nations, and the whole series of events certainly brought it much international discredit. The Germans saw in the poor performance of the Red Army in the early stages of the fighting a confirmation of their own view of it as hopelessly incompetent, and they paid no attention to the fact that Red Army men frequently continued to fight with determination under the most difficult circumstances. The possibility that the British might utilize support for the Finns to occupy Norway reinforced Hitler's agreement with Admiral Raeder's arguments for a German invasion of that country.

The German planning for the invasion of Denmark and Norway was simultaneously simple and complicated. It was simple in the sense that there would be no declaration of war but merely a surprise attack on two neutral countries, neither of which had taken part in the preceding war. German warships and troop transports would carry soldiers who, together with some parachutists, would quickly seize key points in Norway, while a ship with troops would simply enter the Danish port and capital of Copenhagen. The Danish and Norwegian governments would be told to surrender; and the two countries, both or either if one did not surrender, would be crushed in subsequent fighting. The complicated parts of the plan related to the invasion of Norway. The very long coast of that country meant that assaults would be needed at considerable distances from each other. That raised two difficulties. First, almost all the German surface navy would be needed to carry and escort the forces to their destination and would thus be exposed to the British navy that could be expected to do what it could to interfere with German operations. Second, the port of Narvik was both especially important because that was where the railway from the Swedish iron mines terminated, but was also the furthest removed from German bases (Map 2). On the first of these problems, the German navy would just have to take its chances in naval warfare, which turned out to lead to even greater losses than had been anticipated. On the second, there were two forms of assistance expected to make the German task easier. A Norwegian officer in an important position in Narvik was sympathetic to Germany as a follower of the Norwegian traitor Vidkun Quisling who was in touch with Germany, and could be expected to assist the German landing force. Furthermore, the base provided by the Soviets on the Arctic Ocean coast offered a port from which supply and other ships could reach Narvik from the other direction without any likely interference from the British navy.

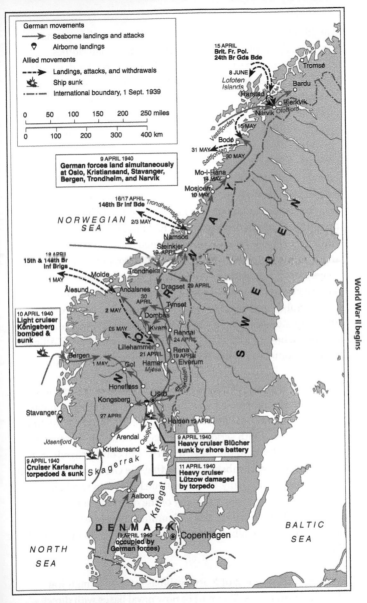

German movements
→ Seaborne landings and attacks
⬥ Airborne landings

Allied movements
--→ Landings, attacks, and withdrawals
💥 Ship sunk
—··— International boundary, 1 Sept. 1939

0   50   100   150   200   250 miles
0   100   200   300   400 km

9 APRIL 1940
German forces land simultaneously at Oslo, Kristiansand, Stavanger, Bergen, Trondheim, and Narvik

16/17 APRIL
146th Br Inf Bde

19 APRIL
15th & 146th Br Inf Brigs

10 APRIL 1940
Light cruiser Königsberg bombed & sunk

9 APRIL 1940
Cruiser Karlsruhe torpedoed & sunk

9 APRIL 1940
Heavy cruiser Blücher sunk by shore battery

11 APRIL 1940
Heavy cruiser Lützow damaged by torpedo

15 APRIL
Brit. Fr. Pol.
24th Br Gds Bde

8 JUNE
Lofoten
Islands

Tromsø
Bardu
Harstad
Bjerkvik
Narvik
Ofotfjord

Vestfjorden
15 MAY
Bodø
31 MAY
Saltfjorden
30 MAY
Mo-i-Rana
14 MAY
Mosjøen
10 MAY

NORWEGIAN SEA

Trondheimsfjord
2/3 MAY
Namsos
Steinkjer
19 APRIL

Molde
1 MAY
Ålesund
Andalsnes
30 APRIL
2 MAY
Dombås
05 MAY
Kvam
Lillehammer
21 APRIL
Gol
1 MAY
Hamar
Mjøsa
Honefoss
Kongsberg
27 APRIL
Stavanger
Jøsenfjord
Arendal
Kristiansand

Trondheim
Dragset
29 APRIL
Tynset
Rendal
24 APRIL
Rena
19 APRIL
Elverum

N O R W A Y

S W E D E N

Bergen
OSLO
Halden 12 APRIL

Skagerrak
Oslofjord

Aalborg

D E N M A R K
(9 APRIL 1940
occupied by
German forces)
Copenhagen

Kattegat

NORTH
SEA

BALTIC
SEA

World War II begins

2. Norwegian campaign

29

The ships with the attacking forces and the escorts left German ports in early April while German officers in civilian clothes travelled to Copenhagen and Oslo to deliver surrender demands. The Danes surrendered immediately, but the Norwegian government did not. The German association with Quisling helped at Narvik, but it served to arouse the majority of Norwegians against Germany. The new German heavy cruiser *Bluecher* was sunk as it sailed up the fjord to the capital Oslo, and the Norwegian government left the city, subsequently to move to England. German forces landed successfully at the key city of Trondheim and seized airfields there and at other places in the country. However, the force that landed at Narvik was in trouble as the British navy immobilized the ten destroyers that had brought them. An Allied landing force took the town but evacuated it after the Germans struck in the west in May 1940. The British, French, and Polish troops landed at two places not far from Trondheim, but both were poorly commanded and without air cover. German control of the air and general disorganization on the Allied side was decisive in the fighting in southern Norway. This led to another government-in-exile in London; however there were important positives for the Allies resulting from the German conquest of Norway.

During the campaign for Norway, the British navy lost an aircraft carrier and several smaller warships, but it was the German navy that suffered most heavily. The two battleships, *Scharnhorst* and *Gneisenau*, were both seriously damaged by torpedoes; several cruisers in addition to the *Bluecher* were sunk or damaged; and the only warships of substantial size that the German navy had left ready for action on 1 July 1940 were one heavy and two light cruisers and four destroyers. Many of the damaged ships were repaired, but at the critical time of summer 1940 the German naval force was not substantial enough to support an invasion of England.

However, the conquest of Norway did assist the German war effort in several ways. There were now naval bases with direct

access to the Atlantic Ocean. When Germany invaded the
Soviet Union, there would be both a base for an attack toward
the Soviet naval base at Murmansk and excellent facilities for air
and sea interference with efforts by the British, and later also the
Americans, to send ships with aid to the Soviet Union by the
northern route. Finally, German control of Norway made it easy to
pressurize Sweden into offering even more assistance to the
German war effort, not only in sending shipments of iron on
Swedish ships but also in allowing German troops and supplies to
utilize the Swedish railway system. Fear of the Swedes dynamiting
the iron mines restrained Germany from invading the country, but
the assumption was that, after victory in the war, this would be
another easily conquered country. Plans for this conquest were
indeed made during the war, but instead the troops in Norway
were held ready to meet an Allied invasion, which the Germans
periodically expected for the rest of the war.

At the time of the occupation of Denmark and the fighting in
Norway, the Germans gave little or no attention to the two
territories associated with Denmark: Iceland and Greenland.
Instead, the British moved to occupy Iceland and President
Roosevelt declared Greenland to be in the Western hemisphere.
These steps would assist the Allies in the Battle of the Atlantic in
subsequent years. However, in 1940, the Germans just did not have
the naval and shipping resources to even consider seizing these
territories, which would be of such importance in the wider war.

The Allied defeat in Norway led directly to the resignation of
Neville Chamberlain as prime minister of Britain. Lord Halifax was
then the preferred candidate in the governing Conservative party to
take over the position. However, he did not think it feasible to lead a
government in a critical time of war from the House of Lords, and
so he declined the position. Consequently, Winston Churchill
became prime minister—despite, as First Lord of the Admiralty,
bearing a large share of the responsibility for the mishandling of the
Norwegian campaign. The new government, which took office on

10 May, the day of the German attack in the west, was a coalition of the Conservative, Labour, and Liberal parties. This coalition government, with very few personnel changes, directed the British government for most of the rest of the war.

One further facet of the winter 1939–40 must be mentioned because it had major repercussions on subsequent developments. There had been a variety of secret diplomatic contacts between elements in Germany and the British government about the possibility of offering a fair peace settlement to Germany if opponents of the Hitler regime inside Germany could succeed in overthrowing Hitler. The British and French governments were united in answering that Germany could get peace, but that Czechoslovakia and Poland would have to be returned to independence. Whatever the differences from the Hitler regime that may have been seen in the Germans involved in these negotiations, there were two points of supreme importance to the Allies. The obvious one was that there was no attempted overthrow of the Hitler government until July 1944. And the other, which may not have been seen as an obvious detraction to these opponents of Hitler inside Germany, but which had a significant impact on the thinking about Germany in the British government, was that some of those who were supposed to have been willing to take part in a coup against Hitler had been involved nonetheless in the planning for and the execution of invasions of a series of neutral countries. These two observations led to the loss of any credibility these internal opponents of the Hitler regime may have had with the Allied negotiators. The conclusion that the new prime minister—who knew of and had agreed to the earlier contacts—and others in the British government drew was that there should be no further negotiations until there had actually been a coup. Should there be a coup, then they would decide on the best policy to follow.

Chapter 3
War in the West: 1940

War plans

Hitler had originally hoped to strike in the West in the late autumn of 1939. Postponements into the spring of 1940 had three major effects on that offensive. First, the time could be and was utilized by the Germans to remedy some of the problems encountered in the campaign against Poland, while neither the French nor the British drew lessons from what had happened. Second, repeated warnings of the forthcoming offensive by opponents of the Hitler regime in Germany, especially Colonel Hans Oster in the intelligence section of the High Command of the Armed Forces (OKW), had the unintended effect of having the last—and accurate—warning essentially disregarded. Third, the time interval was used for a major reorientation of the planned German offensive that interacted fatally with the plans of the French and British to cope with any German attack.

As early as May 1938, Hitler had told his military advisors that a drive in the West would be launched through the Low Countries. The original plan for the 1939 offensive provided that, unlike in 1914, when the Germans had invaded Belgium and Luxembourg, this time Holland would also be invaded. There would be a strong right flank, but its main aim would be to seize ports and bases for the future war against Britain rather than the encirclement of French forces that had been a key feature of the 1914 plan. In the meantime, the Dutch and Belgian governments were refusing to coordinate their defensive efforts with the French and British for fear of provoking Germany. As a consequence, the Allies decided to move forward to assist the Low Countries after they had been attacked. Based on plans containing a portion of the German attack order extracted from an officer in a crashed German plane, the Allies assumed that the Germans would move as they had originally intended. Because of the refusal of the Low Countries to coordinate strategy, the Allies would have to send the most motorized units forward if they expected to stop the Germans before they drove into France. Furthermore, as a part of the concept of keeping the Germans as far away from France as possible, the French commander-in-chief, General Maurice Gamelin, decided that the main French reserve, the French 7th Army, should be sent into Holland at the left flank of the forces sent to rescue the attacked neutrals. As if this did not denude France sufficiently of units that might be moved in an emergency, he also assigned half of all French forces to the Maginot Line of fixed defences built in prior years along the border with Germany.

However, during the interval created by the postponements, the Germans changed their plan. Instead of a strong right flank of the invading force, they decided to strike through the Ardennes and head for the English Channel, in the process cutting off any French and British forces coming to the aid of the Dutch and Belgians. The latter two countries would then be forced to surrender unconditionally by a combination of tricks: parachutists would seize key points before they could be properly manned and defended; German soldiers in Dutch uniforms would confuse whatever defence the Dutch might put up; and heavy bombing of cities and substantial shooting of civilians was expected to demoralize the population as well as the military.

34

The German victory in the West

The German forces struck on 10 May, seizing key Belgian fortifications by parachutists and concentrating armoured units and motorized infantry for a breakthrough in the Ardennes for an early crossing of the Meuse river which was attained already on 13 May. A combination of tanks and motorized infantry pushed through to the Channel, reaching it during the night of 20–21 May (Map 3a and b). By this time, the Dutch had surrendered unconditionally, with the government moving to London and much of the city of Rotterdam devastated by a German air raid. It was this event that was key in the British decision to lift restrictions on the Royal Air Force, allowing it to start bombing German cities. The Allied efforts to counter the German breakthrough had failed, largely due to the faulty allocation of French forces and to a hopelessly disorganized command structure between the Western Allies and within the French forces. Belgium, despite having mobilized substantial forces, many of whom had fought effectively, also surrendered unconditionally on 28 May. This further weakened the Allied forces that had rushed to their aid and consequently been cut off by the German advance to the Channel.

The French command tried to create a new front across northern France, below the German breakthrough. Very worried about the possibility that this would, as in World War I, lead to positional warfare on a front of hundreds of miles, the German commander of the army group that had broken through, General von Rundstedt, with Hitler's agreement on 24 May halted the armoured units striking toward the ports remaining under British and French control so that they could be refreshed and repaired for the thrust south through any new French defensive front. Hitler relied on the promise of Hermann Göring, commander of the German air force, that this force, which had done much to assist the advance up to then, could destroy the cut off Allied units. Effective defensive fighting, the massive deployment of all sorts of ships, and the British air force flying from home bases,

World War II

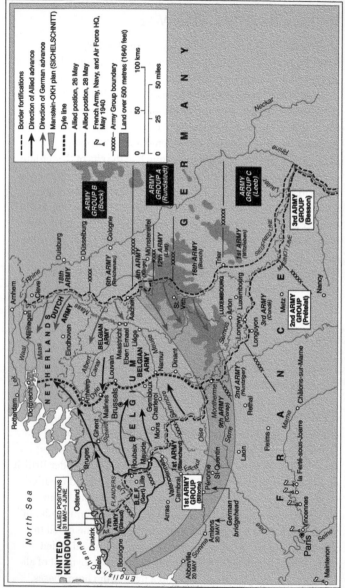

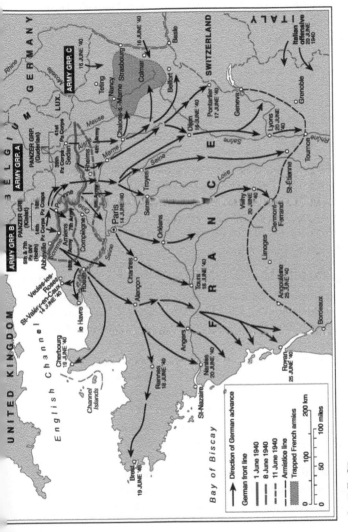

3b. Fall of France

combined with the temporary halt of the German armoured force, to make possible the evacuation of over 200,000 British and over 100,000 French soldiers from the beaches of Dunkirk. Their equipment was left behind, but a key part of Britain's army survived.

The new commander of the French forces, General Maxime Weygand, tried to organize the new defensive line and hoped that evacuated troops from the cut off forces in the north would reinforce it once re-equipped and reorganized in England. Well before that development could occur, the Germans struck the line on 5 June. After a few days of heavy fighting, the Germans broke through, occupied Paris on 14 June, and drove on in spite of the fact that a few French units fought bravely. In those days of June German army units began to massacre French soldiers from the African colonies who had surrendered, another step in the army's descent from the gutter in Poland into the sewer of subsequent campaigns.

In the context of an apparently swift German victory in the West, governments around the world had to make new decisions. This looked to Benito Mussolini like the time to join Germany in war against France and Britain if Italy were to obtain any of the spoils of a war that he imagined had been won. Although Italy was not prepared for a major conflict, he now declared war on the country's World War I allies, had a small attack mounted in the Alps against the French, and in a minimal way initiated campaigns in north and northeast Africa. Francisco Franco, who had completed his conquest of Spain in April 1939, also contemplated entering on Germany's side, but he wanted to make sure of Spanish gains before rather than after joining hostilities. He would aid Germany in many ways, but since neither then nor later could he obtain from Hitler an absolute assurance of full control of the areas he wanted, he had Spain remain nominally neutral.

The Soviet Union had been willing to assist the German occupation of Norway and was enthusiastic about the German offensive in the West. As that campaign appeared to be stunningly successful, the Moscow regime assumed that this was the time to gather in its due under the agreement with Germany. The three Baltic states were occupied and then annexed with any remaining people of German background allowed to leave. New pressures were exerted on Finland, and Romania was obliged to cede both Bessarabia and a part of the Bucovina. As already mentioned, all of Lithuania, including the piece promised to Germany, was taken, and there were arguments between Moscow and Berlin about the demands on Finland and the extent of the territorial demands on Romania, but these issues were settled diplomatically. The critical point that Stalin did not grasp was that these steps of the Soviet Union made the new decisions of the German government easier to implement.

The French government moved to Bordeaux as in 1914, but a new leadership of Marshal Philippe Pétain and Pierre Laval was determined to take the country out of the war rather than fight on from its colonial empire utilizing the essentially untouched French fleet. They asked for an armistice through Spain, and Hitler was quite willing to offer terms since he had at the time no way to seize the French colonial empire, preferred not to have the French fleet continue fighting, assumed that Britain could be crushed easily, and, as will be reviewed, was already interested in 1940 in moving forces to the East to invade the Soviet Union. Under these circumstances he restrained Mussolini's demands on the French, settled on occupying the majority of France including all of its Channel and Atlantic coast, and left a part of the country temporarily unoccupied but defenceless under Pétain. The latter hoped for a place for France which would be internally recast along autocratic lines in a German-dominated Europe. The Germans were never interested in cooperating with the new French regime, but that did not discourage him; and the forces allowed to his government inside unoccupied France and in colonies loyal to his government established in the resort town of Vichy had instructions never to fight the Germans, Italians, or Japanese but always to fight the British, the French, or later any Americans who might join them. A German–French and an Italian–French armistice went into effect the night of 24–25 June 1940, with over a million French soldiers being held as prisoners by the Germans. A small number of Frenchmen joined the recently promoted General Charles de Gaulle in what came to be known as the Free French movement, to which several French colonies in central Africa and the South Pacific rallied in subsequent months, while the Vichy regime arranged for the delivery of Belgium's gold reserves from West Africa to the Germans.

The British government had tried hard, with Churchill personally playing a central role, to persuade the French to continue fighting. In addition to an earlier treaty which committed the two countries not to sign a separate peace treaty, the London government decided positively on a project for them to merge into one in this emergency, but the new regime in France did not even consider this idea. The British government took little time to make its decision in this difficult situation. They would fight on against Germany and Italy from the United Kingdom as long as possible and from the commonwealth and empire if necessary. The escape of the bulk of the country's professional officer corps and numerous soldiers from Dunkirk encouraged this position, which was reinforced by a solid home front that the beginnings of German bombing hardened rather than softened. The government expected a German invasion, mobilized a Home Guard of older men to assist in defending the country, and agreed to a proposal of the chief of the imperial general staff, Field Marshal Sir John Dill, to use poison gas on any German forces that made it ashore. Against the possibility of German occupation of part or all of the home islands, the government sent its gold and foreign exchange reserves to Toronto and Montreal, and initiated preparations for guerrilla warfare in any occupied parts of Britain while the government continued to direct the war from Canada.

It is possible that the Duke of Windsor, the former King Edward VIII, thought of playing a role similar to that of Pétain in France and that World War I prime minister, David Lloyd George, expected to imitate Laval, but the three British political parties were represented in a cabinet that instead looked forward to an eventual victory over Germany by a combination of bombing, blockade, and an expeditionary force to assist the peoples of the lands occupied by Germany as they rose against the Germans who were certain to exploit and antagonize them. The Duke was sent off to the Bahamas, and Lloyd George remained an isolated voice in Parliament. By 19 July when Hitler suggested that peace be made, all the critical decisions had been made in London, and foreign secretary Lord Halifax publicly announced the rejection of peace with Germany.

The British government had earlier insisted that the French fleet move to British ports if France were to be relieved of its obligation not to sign a separate peace treaty. When the Vichy government refused, the British either disarmed French warships or, when those in north Africa refused to move to the French West Indies, destroyed them by naval gunfire. It was a sad end to an alliance, but the London government could neither depend on French or German assurances about those ships nor defend itself against invasion if Germany added the French fleet to Italy's and their own. It was in this connection that the losses and damage to German warships in the Norwegian campaign proved to be critical. Furthermore, as the Germans planned to invade England, complete control of the air was as essential for them as it would be for the Allies in 1944.

The reaction of the USA

The dramatic events of the spring and early summer of 1940 in Western Europe had major effects on the United States. With a presidential election due that year, Franklin Roosevelt, against his prior inclination, decided to run for a third term and, also against the prior and subsequent practice of the country, created something of a coalition government by drawing prominent Republicans into high offices in the administration. There had been minimal changes in the country's neutrality laws, and in spite of endless and very vehement debate, there would be more. At the end of 1938 the president had called for the building up of a real air force. With dangers facing the country both across the Atlantic and the Pacific, he asked Congress for funds for a 'two-ocean navy', and these were voted in July 1940. In the autumn, a majority of Congress agreed that the country needed a substantial rather than a tiny army and instituted the first peacetime draft. While that army was almost dissolved a year later, it did begin to grow and acquire a minimal quantity of modern weapons. France and Britain had placed large orders for military equipment with American factories, and Britain took over the French contracts. Since these were under the 'cash and carry' provision of the amended neutrality laws, British cash dwindled rapidly as deliveries increased. This process led at the end of the year to a plea from Churchill to Roosevelt and, in turn, to the latter's proposal of the Lend-Lease system passed by Congress in March 1941.

Unlike some of his advisors, the president was confident in the summer of 1940 that Britain would hold out, and he moved as far as the law allowed to assist the struggling island. Roosevelt had some remaining surplus World War I weapons shipped to England, and these helped arm the Home Guard. He arranged an exchange of 50 over-age destroyers for 99-year leases on bases for the United States in British possessions in the Western hemisphere, an arrangement shown to the public as enhancing the country's security at a time of great danger. There was much bitter debate about this and related issues in the United States, but voters in November 1940 gave Roosevelt an unprecedented third term. In one respect the German effort to crush Britain in 1940 made some Americans favorable to aiding that country as they saw newsreels and heard radio reports on Germany's attempt to level London.

The German victory had major implications for that country's domestic situation as well as leading to new decisions in the military field. The most important domestic effect was a solidification of the public behind the Nazi regime. At a time when the memory of the lengthy and bloody fighting of World War I in the West was much on people's minds, the appearance of rapid total victory with comparatively minimal losses redounded to the regime's benefit. In addition to this impact on the public there was its effect on the German military. On top of Hitler's massive programme of bribing the higher levels of the army, navy, and air force by secret, tax-free payments, the victory over France brought the generals and admirals promotions and a sense of confidence in Hitler's judgement. The way in which Germany held together for the rest of World War II cannot be understood without this spectacular reinforcement of existing support for the Nazi regime, now enhanced by enthusiasm over a victory identified with Adolf Hitler personally.

The German decision to invade the Soviet Union

Even before the signing of the armistice with France, both Hitler and army chief-of-staff General Franz Halder began planning for an invasion of the Soviet Union. Victory in the West was the assumed prerequisite for the conquest of living space from the Soviet Union in the East, and the first expectation was that this operation could be launched in the autumn of 1940 and completed successfully that year. This issue is reviewed in more detail below, but Germany's leaders also had to address the continued resistance of Britain. An invasion of the south coast of England was planned with tens of thousands of soldiers—assisted by thousands of horses—landing at selected beaches. A list of those to be arrested was printed, and a person was designated to be police chief of London. The needed control of the air was to be secured by the German air force.

The Battle of Britain, as it came to be called, in late June, July, August, and the first half of September produced the first major

German defeat of the war. Although losses on both sides were substantial, the Royal Air Force held on, supported by a population that could not be stampeded into demanding peace. The fighter planes ordered by the Chamberlain government and directed by Air Marshal Dowding, assisted by radar, spotters, and anti-aircraft guns, were obviously not crushed by mid-September 1940. After that date, the weather in the Channel became too rough for any invasion attempt. With invasion off for the year, massive bombing of British cities through the winter caused substantial damage and casualties, but it did not break the morale of the population. Instead it encouraged that of the British army, which was being reorganized and rearmed, with the establishment of commandoes to raid the German-controlled coast, and the sense of a possible reversal of fortune in some people in German-occupied areas as they saw British planes flying overhead to bomb first the invasion preparations on the coast and then targets within Germany itself.

If Germany's defeat in the Battle of Britain obliged Hitler to defer invasion of England to 1941, other problems had the same effect on his hope of invading the Soviet Union in 1940. Vast numbers of German forces had to be moved from the West to the eastern areas of Germany and occupied Poland. Equipment had to be repaired and increased. Casualties incurred in the campaign in the West and losses of planes, tanks, and other weapons had to be made good. It was also essential to make significant improvements in the transport and storage facilities in the eastern areas where massive German forces were to be based and from which their advance eastwards would have to be supplied. By the end of July 1940, Hitler recognized that when these needed preparations were completed, it would be too close to the start of winter for a single season campaign in 1940; that also had to be postponed until the spring of 1941. Its anticipated rapid success would discourage the British while encouraging the Japanese to move forward in east Asia and thereby divert the Americans from any activity in Europe until Germany was ready to attack them. German planning for the campaign in the East was well under way by August 1940, and this is reviewed in Chapter 4. Already in August 1940, diplomatic portions of those preparations affected the international situation. Germany reversed its policy toward Finland, now expecting it to assist in the attack on the Soviet Union instead of being absorbed by it. The territorial dispute between Hungary and Romania was also resolved by Germany, which thereupon guaranteed Romania, sent troops there, and expected it to participate in the invasion of the Soviet Union.

The Soviet leadership noted such changes in German policy and in November sent foreign commissar Vyacheslav Molotov to Berlin to arrange a new agreement. Nothing came of this, but Stalin still refused to believe that Germany intended to attack them. Neither a copy of Hitler's invasion directive of December 1940, obtained by Soviet intelligence, nor a summary of it that an opponent of Hitler's had provided to the Americans and that Roosevelt had transmitted to Stalin in February 1941, awakened the Soviet leader. He was determined to continue supplying critical materials to Germany, to not alerting his country's armed forces, and to not interfering with German aerial reconnaissance over the Soviet Union that began in October 1940.

The war in Africa and the Middle East

While the Germans were bombing Britain and preparing the attack on the Soviet Union, Mussolini had Italian forces move in a small way in Africa. In northeast Africa, Italian troops occupied the small British colony of British Somaliland. Thereafter, however, the Italian army in Eritrea, Italian Somaliland, and occupied Ethiopia was unable to resist British forces striking from Kenya in February 1941. The Italian troops were defeated and either captured or besieged in isolated garrisons. The exiled Emperor Haile Selassie returned to Addis Ababa, and in April 1941, Roosevelt declared the Red Sea no longer a war zone so that American ships with supplies for the British army in Egypt could move around the Cape of Good Hope and unload at the Suez Canal. By that time, the American president had also established an air supply route for the British in the Middle East that ran from Takoradi on the west coast of Africa across the French colonies that had rallied to de Gaulle.

In the meantime, Italy had suffered a series of other military defeats. The Germans had firmly told Mussolini that they wanted the Balkans kept quiet. When he learned that German troops were being sent to Romania, he concluded that this had been done so that Germany could pre-empt any other country from a major role in the area, whether the Soviet Union or Italy. To assert Italy's role, he ordered an invasion of Greece at the end of October 1940, without consulting Berlin any more than Berlin had checked with Rome before sending troops into Romania. The difference was that the Romanians expected to fight against the Soviet Union alongside Germany to regain land ceded to the Soviets—and perhaps some more—while the Greeks fought against the Italians to retain their independence. Minimally assisted by the British, who defeated an Italian fleet at the Battle of Cape Matapan in March 1941, the Greeks fought effectively and drove the Italians back into Albania, which Italy had occupied in 1939. In addition, the Italian forces in north Africa were also being defeated.

The Italian army in Libya was as poorly led and prepared as that which had invaded Greece. There was a short advance into Egypt, and then the Italians sat down while the British built up their forces. In spite of the danger to the home islands, Churchill had insisted on sending reinforcements and equipment to Egypt. On 11 November 1940, British planes damaged several Italian battleships in Taranto harbour, thus interfering with Italy's naval possibilities in the Mediterranean. On 9 December, the British attacked the Italian army in Egypt, surprised and defeated it, and drove the 60 miles to the Egyptian–Libyan border. In early January the British struck again and in that and the following month destroyed the Italian army at Beda Fromm, capturing over

100,000 men. The British advance came to what could have been a temporary halt at El Agheila. The possibility of seizing the rest of Libya in 1941 was aborted by the German reaction to the Italian defeats and, in turn, the British reaction to steps Germany took to rescue its Italian ally.

The Italian military failures in Greece and Africa confronted the German leadership with two practical problems. If all of Italy's colonial empire were lost as looked increasingly likely, this might lead to an overthrow of Mussolini's regime. Hitler was very much concerned about this and renewed his earlier offer of a military expeditionary force to be sent to Libya. What Mussolini had earlier rejected he now accepted. This is the origin of the German Africa Corps led by one of Hitler's favourite generals, Erwin Rommel, being sent to north Africa in February 1941 to help defend Libya and advance into Egypt.

The other danger in Italy's situation as seen from Berlin was the possibility of British planes from Greek bases attacking the Romanian oilfields critical for Germany's war effort. The best way for the Germans to cope with this problem was for German forces to attack Greece from Bulgaria and perhaps southern Yugoslavia, precisely the border areas the Greeks had denuded of troops to halt the Italian invasion. Obtaining the agreement of Bulgaria was expected to prove easy and was so: they were promised Greek territory to provide a coast on the Aegean Sea lost after World War I. It looked for a short time that Germany could reach an agreement with Yugoslavia also, but this was aborted by a coup in Belgrade on 27 March 1941, which replaced the government that had signed a deal with Germany. Hitler thereupon decided to attack Yugoslavia as well as Greece.

On Sunday, 6 April 1941, the Germans opened their campaign with a massive bombing of the Yugoslav capital of Belgrade and rapid advances into that country and Greece (Maps 4a and b). The invasion of Yugoslavia was designed not only to conquer that

World War II

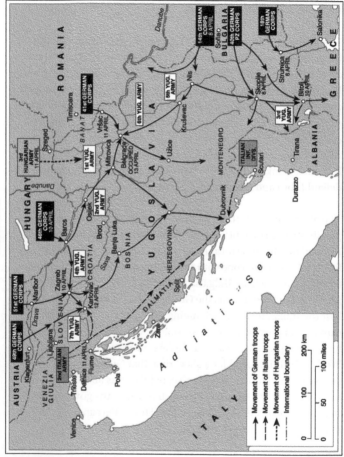

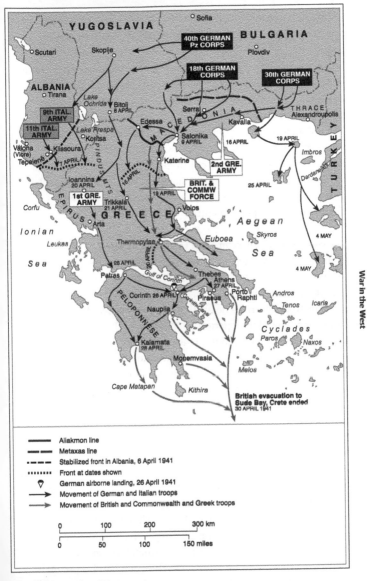

Key:

- ──────── Aliakmon line
- ── ── ── Metaxas line
- ── ─ ── ─ Stabilized front in Albania, 6 April 1941
- ·········· Front at dates shown
- ▽ German airborne landing, 26 April 1941
- ──▷ Movement of German and Italian troops
- ──▶ Movement of British and Commonwealth and Greek troops

```
0        100        200        300 km
0        50         100        150 miles
```

4b. Balkan campaign

country but to prevent a repeat of the withdrawal south of the country's army as had happened in World War I. In this the Germans were successful, and they drew in Italy, Hungary, and Bulgaria to end the fighting there quickly by offering each a piece of the country (from which Germany also annexed a part). The area would, however, not become as quiet as the Germans had hoped, and resistance forces required the stationing of German and Italian forces in subsequent years. The Germans also succeeded in driving into northern Greece and evicting the small British force that had been sent there. Air superiority and rapid advances by armoured columns supported by parachutists at key points made for a relatively quick and successful German occupation of the whole country.

The conquest of Greece opened the possibility of an assault on the island of Crete. A combined parachute and surface ship invasion succeeded against substantial British resistance. Once again Britain had to evacuate a force, but the casualties among German airborne troops were so heavy that Germany ordered no subsequent parachute operations in the war. The German–Italian attacks on the island of Malta tried that base for British planes and submarines severely, but the abstention from any employment of an airborne force to help seize the island meant that Axis plans for trying to do so could never be implemented. Although convoys to resupply and rearm Malta suffered substantial losses, the island continued to provide a base for Britain's campaigns in the Mediterranean.

For a short time it looked as if everything in that theatre might fall to the Axis. Rommel attacked in Libya at the end of March and quickly drove the British back into Egypt. Unable to take the port city of Tobruk, he was halted as the British reorganized units evacuated from Greece and Crete. They were, however, unable to defeat Rommel's combined Italian–German force in their 'Battleaxe' offensive in mid-June. On the other hand, a pro-Axis rebellion in Iraq in April was crushed by British forces, primarily from India, in May. The Iraqi leader, Rashid Ali al-Gaylani, fled to Germany where, like the Palestinian Arab nationalist, Haj Amin al-Husayni, he hoped for help to drive the British out of the Middle East, never recognizing that German or Italian rule was likely to be harsher than British dominance. The little help Germany could provide to the revolt in Iraq was sent via the French Mandate of Syria where the Vichy authorities did whatever they could to help Germany. This provoked the British into invading Syria on 8 June. Unlike their failing stand against the Germans the preceding year, the French force in Syria fought steadily against Australian, British, Free French, and Indian troops until a 14 July armistice. The Germans could not provide substantial help because of their concentration on the invasion of the Soviet Union, which, in German planning, was to be followed, not preceded, by the taking of the Middle East. The British turned Syria over to de Gaulle once it was clear that there was no immediate danger of a major German push into the area. An important subsequent effect of British victories in Iraq and Syria was that what became the southern route of supplies to the Soviet Union remained in Allied hands instead of the dangerous alternative: an Axis base threatening the Caucasus from the south.

Chapter 4
Barbarossa: the German invasion of the Soviet Union

Planning for the invasion of the Soviet Union and the Holocaust

While German planning for the invasion of the Soviet Union began in the summer of 1940, it became clear to Hitler that preparations could not be advanced quickly enough for the short campaign that he expected to be completed in 1940 before the winter set in. On 31 July 1940, he informed his top military advisors that the invasion would take place in the spring of 1941. Practical preparations such as improvements in transport and supply provisions in east Prussia and the German-controlled areas in Poland as well as the transfer of troops from the West were initiated immediately. Planning in German military headquarters in the summer and autumn of 1940 and the first months of 1941 was based on several assumptions, most of which turned out to be mistaken. It was assumed that the campaign would be over before the winter of 1941–2; and that the first sharp blows would produce a total collapse of the regime. However, the poor performance of the Red Army in the 1939–40 winter war against Finland obscured the fact that large numbers of Red Army soldiers had continued to fight hard under the most difficult situations and reinforced the prior under-estimation of the soldiers Germany and its allies would face. In spite of an implicit hint from the Soviet side, when their visiting commission had asked to see where Germans made their *big* tanks on being shown the factory where the German Mark IV tank was made, the Germans assumed that the Mark IV tank, then the largest in their inventory, would be adequate for the campaign against Soviet armour and infantry. Captured French and confiscated Czechoslovakian tanks would be utilized on a substantial scale, as would a variety of German and seized non-German trucks. Little attention was paid to the logistics issue of spare parts and repair facilities for this great variety of armoured vehicles and trucks that might be needed in a campaign that was to cover large distances with few and generally poor roads. Since the expected quick victory over the Soviet Union was to be followed by an advance into the Middle East, replacement tanks were to be sent to the army in the East only after victory over the Red Army, and so these had been painted in desert camouflage.

Diplomatic preparations for the invasion of the Soviet Union included the involvement of Finland and Romania on Germany's side. It was correctly assumed that both would want to recover the territory they had been obliged to cede to the Soviets and perhaps take some more from a defeated enemy. Neutral Sweden was persuaded to allow the transit of German troops not only to and from occupied Norway but also when these were to participate in the invasion at the northern end of the Finnish–Soviet front. That front would be met by one German army group thrusting through the Baltic states towards Leningrad, while a larger army group would strike at the central portion of the front towards and beyond Moscow. In the south, a third army group assisted by substantial Romanian troops would conquer the Ukraine with its agricultural and industrial riches and then seize the Caucasus region with its oil.

In connection with the planning for Romania's role in the coming campaign, Hitler personally explained to Romania's leader, Marshal Ion Antonescu, an important objective of the invasion. Asked at their meeting, on 12 June 1941, what was to happen to the large numbers of Jews in the areas that advancing Romanian and German troops would occupy, Hitler explained that they were to be killed. By the time of the meeting, extensive preparations were under way to organize and orient for this task special units of

the German security police and the uniformed 'order police' as
well as some other units who were to accompany and follow the
German army and systematically kill all Jews in the Soviet Union.
In the rapid forward rush of the invading forces, there would be
local variations and problems in this; but with the full support of
an army that was winning in what looked to Hitler and army
chief-of-staff Halder like a successful campaign, by the end of July
he had decided to extend the systematic killing programme to all
of Europe. The resumed advance in October may have played a
part in his assuring the leader of the radical Palestinian Arabs, Haj
Amin al-Husseinie, in November that the killing programme
would be extended to the whole world.

Germany invades the Soviet Union

The Germans attacked the Soviet Union in the early hours of
22 June 1941, with an army of over three million men and over
600,000 horses and about half a million men in the armies of
Romania and Finland. The German air force struck Soviet airfields
and the few Soviet planes that had got off the ground, destroying
several thousand in the first few days and securing control of the air
for the early phase of the campaign. Stalin's errors made for easy
early German victories. The purges of experienced officers in 1937-9
left the Red Army at all levels without enough trained and
experienced officers. The fear of domestic opposition if any portion
of the country were occupied had led to heavy allocation of forces
near the frontline and hence they were susceptible to encirclements.
The westward expansion of the Soviet Union through the
annexations of 1939-40 meant that the old fortifications had been
neglected while there was not enough time for the creation of new
ones. Thus the annexations weakened rather than strengthened
Soviet defensive capability. The unwillingness of Stalin to believe his
own intelligence and that provided him by the American and British
governments not only meant that German air reconnaissance over
the Soviet Union that had taken place months before the invasion
had not been repulsed but that the initial German ground attack was

not resisted in many places because Stalin imagined that such action would provoke a German attack in retaliation. Under these circumstances, German armoured thrusts rapidly drove through major portions of the Red Army in the northern and central portions of the front. Tens of thousands of Red Army soldiers surrendered and large quantities of Soviet equipment fell into German hands. It was this set of early victories that gave both Hitler and army chief-of-staff General Halder the impression that the campaign in the east had essentially been won in the first six weeks (see Map 5).

While the tactical victories of the initial German strike were impressive, several features of the first two months of fighting already pointed to a different outcome, which almost no one in German headquarters realized. On the technical side, there was the appearance of Soviet tanks, the KV-1 and the T 01, which were superior to any Germany tanks. Orders for the development and production of better tanks were issued in Germany that autumn, but the new types, the Mark V Panther and Mark VI Tiger, would not be ready to appear on the battlefield until late 1942 with substantial numbers not to be available until 1943. On the human side, the Germans failed to note that in many cases Red Army men fought tenaciously and sometimes hid in the countryside as German shooting of large numbers of prisoners and even larger numbers of civilians encouraged continued resistance. On the political side, there was what would become for the remainder of the war the critical fact: like Alexander I against Napoleon and unlike Nicholas II and the Provisional Government in World War I, the regime had maintained effective control of the unoccupied portions of the country. This meant that new divisions of troops could be mobilized and sent into battle, that factories could be evacuated while those previously built in the Urals area could continue to produce weapons, and that for several years all losses could be replaced, even as Germany's ability to do so was declining.

It must also be noted that even in the first months of fighting, Germany and its allies were meeting resistance at the northern

— — —	German position, 21 June 1941
11th ARMY	German formation

Approximate front line

———	10 July 1941
··········	16 July 1941
— — —	25 August 1941
▬ ▬ ▬	12 November 1941
▪▪▪▪▪	5 December 1941
	Encirclement battle
xxxxx——	German Army Group boundary
xxxxx — —	Soviet Front (Army Group) boundary
—·—·—	International boundary, 21 June 1941

0   200   400 kms

0   100   200 miles

5. Barbarossa

and southern ends of the front that proved quite serious. In the north, the German force that was to take the Soviet port of Murmansk was unable to do so. It was halted, ironically, at the place substantially west of Murmansk where the Soviets had allowed the German navy to have a base during the years the two countries were allied. Furthermore, even though Finnish armies advanced through the territory ceded to the Soviet Union under the March 1940 peace treaty, they were unable to cut off railway communication from Murmansk to the Russian interior or to meet the German forces striking towards Leningrad. At the southern end of the front, Romanian and German forces had advanced some distance, but they neither caused the Red Army facing them to collapse nor pushed into the Ukraine as rapidly as their leaders had hoped.

The German army group in the north was able to seize Lithuania and Latvia and much of Estonia, but its advance on Leningrad was slowed by Red Army resistance. Since Hitler intended to have the city levelled, he did not want it taken in street fighting, he wanted it to be surrounded and its population and their defenders starved to death. The city was cut off, and there would be mass starvation, but some supplies did get through by water (and in the winter over ice) across Lake Ladoga, and the city held out until fully relieved in January 1944.

In the central part of the front the Germans once more carried out two major breakthrough-and-encirclement battles, which pushed the front beyond Smolensk. The Soviets, however, again established a coherent front as the Germans were ground to a halt, in part due to exhaustion of the troops and in part due to wear as well as losses among the armoured and motorized units. The Red Army not only received substantial additional forces but in local counter-offensives either stopped the Germans or, in a few places like the town of Yelnya, drove them back. Obviously a renewed major German offensive towards Moscow would require the repair of railways and roads for the building up of massive supplies replacing what had been used up in the preceding four months. The inability of the German and Romanian forces in the southern part of the front to push forward as successfully as those in the middle had done would, furthermore, threaten a flanking strike from the south into any resumed German advance towards Moscow; the further it went, the more vulnerable its flank would become. Under these circumstances of enforced delay at the centre, Hitler ordered a strike south from the German central army group to meet a strike north from the army group in the south. Since Stalin refused to heed the advice of his military to withdraw in the face of this operation, what came to be called the battle of Kiev not only lost that city and much of the agricultural and industrial area of the Ukraine but several hundred thousand soldiers as well.

By October, as the Germans prepared for a major push towards Moscow, there were the beginnings of support for the two contending sides. Hungary had entered the war on Germany's side and sent a small force, primarily for fear of Romania becoming too important to Germany. Mussolini did not want to be ignored and sent several divisions to fight alongside the Germans on the southern part of the front. There were also contingents from the puppet states of Croatia and Slovakia, while Francisco Franco, the dictator of Spain, sent what was called the Blue Division. It fought at the northern part of the front and, when returned to Spain under pressure from the Western Allies, would be replaced by the far smaller Spanish Legion. The Germans also recruited volunteers in the parts of Europe they had occupied, and eventually units were put together made up of Ukrainian, Danish, Norwegian, and French volunteers. The last, called the Charlemagne unit, eventually helped defend Berlin in 1945. There were also numerous Ukrainians and other deserters from the Red Army who enrolled on the German side.

The British government decided to assist the Soviet Union the moment it learned of the German invasion. Shipments of military equipment were sent as soon as possible though the quantities were small and would be missing from the needed reinforcement of Malaya. British and Soviet troops occupied Iran so that its north-south railway could be utilized for the sending of aid. That route eventually carried a quarter of American aid (while another quarter went to the northern ports of Murmansk and Archangel and half was shipped or flown across the Pacific). President Roosevelt was more confident that the Soviet Union would endure than his advisors were, and was reinforced in this view by his aide Harry Hopkins whom he sent to Moscow to meet Stalin and to assess the situation. It was at first difficult to persuade the American public that sending aid to Russia was a good idea, but over time this changed. For the public in Britain, there was not only the sense of now having a major ally in the fighting but relief as the German air force shifted from bombing Britain to supporting the German army in the East. The diplomatic and military representatives Britain and the United States sent to the Soviet Union were never treated as well as their German predecessors had been, but in spite of endless difficulties and complaints, the military alliance of the three powers held.

In the first months of German advance and occupation, key features of German policy became clear to the local Soviet population and, of great significance, by rumour and other means would become equally clear to the rest of the Soviet people. The mass killing of civilians, the slaughter of people in hospitals and mental institutions, and the systematic starvation of prisoners of war—with shooting at locals who tried to bring the prisoners food and water—very quickly showed the Soviet people that they were fighting for their lives. Most adults and older people in the newly occupied areas had experienced occupation by the Germans and their allies' armies in the prior war; they could quickly see that while there had been terrible incidents then, this was an entirely different army. Whatever the locals thought about the systematic killing of Jews, most came to realize that they themselves were likely to be next. Many in the Ukraine and Baltic states initially imagined that the Germans would liberate them from an oppressive Soviet rule, but increasingly most came to realize that expropriation and extermination were central German aims. Some in the Ukraine never did realize that while Stalin had wanted them to become good communists, however many of them died in the process, Hitler now planned for them to disappear from the face of the earth—to be replaced by German settlers. However, over time an increasing proportion of the population learned. In the spring of 1942 the Germans calculated that in the first seven months of the fighting, well over two million Red Army prisoners of war had been killed or had died of disease and starvation in German custody, a toll of 10,000 a day, seven days a week. All this occurred in front of the local population. With a few exceptions, no one then knew these statistics, but the basic reality was obvious to all. The German military transformed Stalin from a hated and feared dictator into the benign protector and saviour of the peoples of the Soviet Union.

The Eastern front in the winter of 1941–42

In October and November the Germans launched drives towards Moscow. German units ground forward in some places, but initial substantial advances in some places were offset by minimal advances in others. The foreign embassies were evacuated from Moscow, and detailed plans for the destruction of facilities in the capital and the displacement of government agencies were prepared. The front, however, held, and the Red Army was reinforced as German units were increasingly worn down. No one reading the postwar memoirs of German generals would know this, but it was just as cold and the snow was just as deep for the Red Army as it was for the Germans; the Germans were simply unused to these conditions. Furthermore, the British advances in north Africa obliged the Germans to transfer a whole air fleet to the Mediterranean, thus weakening German air strength on the Eastern front at a critical time.

While the Germans still struggled to inch forward in the centre, the Red Army won local victories at both ends of the front. In the south, the German advance had reached Rostov, the gateway to the Caucasus. A Soviet counter-offensive in late November drove them out of Rostov and to a position further west. In the north, the German force that had reached Tikhvin in hopes of connecting with the Finnish army was similarly driven back. At the front before Moscow, the Germans ground to a halt early in December just as the Soviets were about to launch a major counter-offensive.

Both from Soviet spies in Japan and the obvious absence of a major Japanese build-up in Manchuria, it was clear to Stalin that the Japanese had decided to adhere to the Neutrality Pact they had signed with the Soviet Union in April and instead of joining the Germans by attacking the far eastern provinces of the Soviet Union were about to attack the United States, Britain, and the Netherlands. This meant that most Soviet forces in the Far East, many of them experienced in the earlier fighting with the Japanese, could be brought to Europe and replaced, at least partially, with newly organized formations. Reinforced by divisions from Siberia, the Red Army in early December struck a totally unprepared and exhausted German central front. In some places German soldiers fled in panic, in some they fought hard, but the situation quickly developed into a major Soviet victory. It was not merely that the German advance had been halted and pushed back a little, in several places the Red Army had also broken through German lines, threatening the encirclement of substantial German units, and pushing westwards (Map 6). Unequipped to cope with the weather, German soldiers and equipment froze, and undernourished horses could not pull back much of the equipment through deep snow. However, for two main reasons, this German defeat did not lead to a total collapse of the German front.

While the German military leaders at the front wanted to withdraw to some kind of defensible line, and one of them, General Erich Hoepner, did do so, effectively saving a large force that had been about to be surrounded, Hitler refused this request.

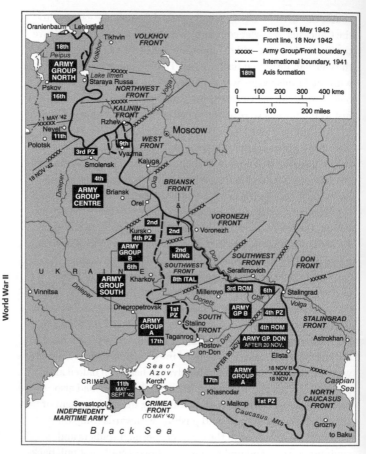

Oranienbaum—Leningrad
Tikhvin
VOLKHOV FRONT
L. Peipus
18th
ARMY GROUP NORTH
Lake Ilmen
Staraya Russa
NORTHWEST FRONT
Pskov
16th
1 MAY '42
Nevel'
11th
Rzhev
KALININ FRONT
Moscow
Polotsk
3rd PZ
9th
WEST FRONT
Vyazma
18 NOV '42
Smolensk
Kaluga
Dnieper
4th
ARMY GROUP CENTRE
Briansk
BRIANSK FRONT
Orel
&
2nd
VORONEZH FRONT
Kursk
4th PZ
2nd
Voronezh
ARMY GROUP B
2nd HUNG
Don
SOUTHWEST FRONT
DON FRONT
6th
Kharkov
8th ITAL
SOUTHWEST FRONT
Serafimovich
UKRAINE
ARMY GROUP SOUTH
Millerovo
3rd ROM
6th
Stalingrad
Vinnitsa
Dnieper
Donets
Chir
Volga
Dnepropetrovsk
1st PZ
SOUTH FRONT
ARMY GP B
4th PZ
STALINGRAD FRONT
ARMY GROUP A
Stalino
4th ROM
17th
Taganrog
Rostov-on-Don
ARMY GP. DON
AFTER 20 NOV.
Astrokhan'
AFTER 20 NOV
Elista
ARMY GROUP A
18 NOV B
18 NOV A
Caspian Sea
Sea of Azov
CRIMEA
Kerch'
11th
MAY-SEPT '42
CRIMEA FRONT
(TO MAY '42)
17th
Khasnodar
1st PZ
NORTH CAUCASUS FRONT
Sevastopol
INDEPENDENT MARITIME ARMY
Maikop
Caucasus Mts
Grozny
to Baku
Black Sea

Legend:
– – – Front line, 1 May 1942
—— Front line, 18 Nov 1942
xxxxx Army Group/Front boundary
–·–·– International boundary, 1941
18th Axis formation

0 100 200 300 400 kms
0 100 200 miles

6. German–Soviet Front, 1941

Hitler was furious about Hoepner's withdrawal, and when told that he could not kick Hoepner out of the army and deprive him of his pension and the right to wear his uniform without a formal court martial, an outraged Hitler decided to have the German parliament meet to strip all Germans of all procedural rights. That would be done by an enthusiastic German parliament when it met for the last time during the Nazi era in April 1942, but this did not alter the crisis at the front in December. On the contrary, Hitler ordered that the troops halt wherever they were and fight from existing positions, even if surrounded. The German front began to hold, although at two places, Cholm and the Demyansk area, they were in surrounded islands. It may be that the success of the German air force in providing them with supplies until the German army could re-establish contact with them in the spring encouraged Hitler to try a similar arrangement with the far larger German force isolated in Stalingrad a year later.

The second main factor, however, that enabled the Germans to hold in the centre and avert disaster was the decision of Stalin to launch offensives on the northern and southern sections of the frontline. Instead of concentrating on a follow-up to the initial victory before Moscow, Stalin now underestimated the Germans in the same way that Hitler had earlier underestimated the Soviets. The Red Army offensives made only minimal gains at considerable cost while the Germans had time to stabilize the centre of the frontline. That front was one that looked most erratic, but it symbolized the total defeat of Germany's hopes of destroying the Soviet Union on the one hand, and the expectation of an exceedingly long and difficult set of campaigns ahead for the Soviets on the other. As fighting continued after the stabilization of the front in March–April 1942, it would remain the place where most of the fighting of World War II occurred.

The unoccupied and the occupied Soviet Union

On the Soviet side of the front, the evacuated industries began to function and deliver products, especially weapons and munitions, for the Red Army. The people worked extremely hard even though working conditions were poor and food shortages developed. Substantial additional army divisions were raised, and the earlier small programme of releasing imprisoned purged officers and generals was expanded. Unlike the other combatant countries, the Soviet Union enrolled hundreds of thousands of women, placing them in combat formations as well as in support roles, including Red Air Force squadrons. With some help from transport planes provided by the United States, the Central Staff of the Partisan Movement provided munitions, officers, and directions to a partisan movement in the German-occupied parts of the country. This tied down German forces in rear area security operations, at critical times it interfered with German transportation and communications, facilitated the collection of intelligence, and reminded the population of the occupied areas that the regime was likely to return and they would be well advised to behave accordingly.

On the German side of the front, a civilian administration headed by Alfred Rosenberg had been prepared beforehand and was installed in territory well behind the front. Nearer the front, there was a system of military administration. In both, there was extensive economic exploitation and the seizing of individuals for slave labour in Germany and elsewhere. So-called anti-partisan operations that included rear area formations and frontline divisions temporarily assigned to the rear in almost all cases turned into mass slaughter of civilians and the burning of communities as the partisans escaped and subsequently found it easier to recruit new members. The Germans were especially enthusiastic about the Soviet system of collective farms which gave the state first call on the crop and hence extended it to the few remaining individual farms. They did recruit some collaborators including former prisoners of war who found this a possible escape from starvation. In a very few places the Germans also began to implement a tiny portion of their plan for massive settlement of German farmers who would eventually displace the allegedly inferior Slavic population, but there was little time for such experiments. High German officers looked forward to receiving huge estates in the East along with their regular bribe money from their beloved leader, but perhaps it would be fair to express doubt that large numbers of ordinary Germans would voluntarily have settled in the armed villages the regime planned to set up. They would presumably have found their names listed for compulsory resettlement in the local newspaper.

Germany turned over to Romania both the land earlier ceded to the Soviet Union and also an additional portion of the Ukraine. This territory, named Transnistria, became a Romanian colony where masses of Jews were murdered and Romanian officials had an opportunity to enrich themselves. Finland also received back the land ceded in the 1940 treaty. The hope of the Finnish government for additional Karelian territory was thwarted not only by the Germans—who intended to annex Finland but had not told them—but also by pressure from the United States, which, unlike Britain, did not declare war on Finland but cautioned the Finns about going too far.

The inability of the Germans to defeat the Soviet Union quickly made the whole war look different. Even the survival of Britain in 1940 had left most in Germany certain of victory and most people outside Germany wondering how Germany could be defeated. Things looked different now and some Germans began to worry about the outcome of the war, while the Allies began to look with more confidence to the future. This change in perspective was strengthened as Japan struck in East Asia and brought the United States into open participation in the war alongside Britain and the Soviet Union.

Chapter 5
Japan expands its war with China

Japan decides to expand its war

Japan had been in open war with China since July 1937. It had rejected the possibility of a negotiated settlement in January 1938, and was continuing a process of occasional advances against Chinese resistance. It never occurred to leaders in Tokyo that it was the constant destruction of Chinese communities, killing and raping of Chinese civilians, and generally abominable behaviour that was slowly but steadily consolidating Chinese opposition and gaining support for the Nationalist government of Chiang Kai-shek. The Japanese took the view that it was supplies from other countries that was keeping the Chinese fighting. Whatever supplies that the Soviet Union provided over land and whatever other countries sent across the Burma Road or the Haiphong–Hanoi railway from French Indo-China were welcomed by the Chinese, but it was not this that caused them to decide to continue fighting—they would have continued to fight regardless, with or without this outside assistance. Because of their focus on the fight with China, German victories in the West in April, May, and June of 1940 looked to the Japanese government as an opportunity to close off much of the outside aid.

For years Japan had tried unsuccessfully by diplomacy to have the French government close the Haiphong–Hanoi railway. Now there appeared to be an alternative; the Japanese army would occupy the northern part of Indo-China and thereby close the route. The Vichy government, to which the French colonial administration was loyal, was agreeable to this request. In September 1940, as Vichy forces fought to keep the British and Free French away from Dakar in French west Africa, Japanese forces quietly occupied northern Indo-China. In view of the dangerous situation Britain was in after Germany's victory in France, the Japanese were able to pressurize the London government into closing the Burma Road for three months. When the three months were up, victory in the Battle of Britain made reopening the road look feasible, and Britain did so.

The leaders in Tokyo did not need the Germans to point out that the defeat of the Netherlands and France made their east Asian colonies attractive targets for the expansion of Japan's empire. Furthermore, Britain's need to defend the home islands against a possible German invasion and to defend its position in the Middle East against Italy in practice made it most difficult, if not impossible, for it to defend its vast possessions in south and southeast Asia and the dominions of Australia and New Zealand. When the Germans pointed this out to Tokyo as a unique opportunity to seize Singapore, the Japanese responded that they planned to do so but in 1946. That was the year when, under legislation passed by the United States' Congress, the United States would give up its bases in the Philippines, which was scheduled to become independent in 1944. The German government realized that the factor restraining Japan was concern about the Americans on the left flank of any southward advance. Since they expected to go to war with the United States anyway, they promised to join Japan in war with the United States as soon as Japan attacked the United States. Germany would then have on its side the major navy it had not yet been able to construct, before the Americans could complete construction of the two-ocean navy Congress had approved. When Japanese foreign minister Matsuoka Yosuke visited Germany in March 1941, Hitler personally repeated this promise.

Debates within the Japanese government revolved around the issue of timing and were influenced by the German invasion of the Soviet Union in June 1941. Rather than joining their German and Italian partners of the September 1940 Tripartite Pact against the Soviets, the Tokyo leaders decided to move south. It was clear to them that since the Soviet Union was fighting for its life, it could neither strike Japan in the back as Japan moved south nor continue to provide substantial aid to the Chinese Nationalists. In July 1941, therefore, Japanese forces occupied the southern part of French Indo-China, clearly moving *away* from concentrating on war with China to preparing attacks on territories controlled by the Netherlands, Britain, and the United States in east and southeast Asia as well as the South Pacific. There were both continued discussion within the Japanese government and detailed preparation for attacks on Malaya, the Dutch East Indies, the Philippines, and other American island possessions in the Pacific. It never occurred to any leaders in Tokyo that conquest of the oil wells, tin mines, and rubber plantations of southeast Asia could not lead to moving these wells, mines, and plantations to the home islands of Japan. It would merely mean Japanese control of the sites, with the need to move their products to the home islands on Japanese ships, without the help of chartered ships of other countries. Of critical significance for the fighting Japan was about to start was, therefore, that no serious preparations had been made either to utilize their own limited shipping efficiently or to protect it from submarine attack.

While the Japanese were preparing their moves and printing occupation currency for the lands to be conquered, the American and British governments were trying to discourage them from attacking their possessions. Unlike the Soviets who had sent supplies to the Germans until minutes before being attacked, the American government had earlier reduced some forms of trade with Japan and had embargoed oil when southern Indo-China was occupied. Knowing that there was no Chinese navy for Japan to fight with, oil was a product needed by Japan for war with Britain, the Netherlands, and the United States. The British and Dutch similarly stopped oil sales to Japan. American leaders, especially President Roosevelt personally and the secretary of state, Cordell Hull, spent countless hours in negotiations with Japanese diplomats in Washington. The latter preferred peace, but the Tokyo government was moving in the opposite direction. It was not influenced by American and British efforts to deter Japan from expanding the war it was already involved in. In their deterrence efforts, the United States had moved a large portion of its fleet to Hawaii and sent the first available B-17 flying fortresses to the Philippines, while Britain ordered the movement of two major warships, a battleship, and a battle-cruiser to Singapore. In the final weeks of talks, the suggestion came up that if Japan would evacuate southern Indo-China, the United States would sell them all the oil they wanted. Japanese diplomats in Washington were immediately instructed not to discuss this possibility—which implied abandonment of expanding the war with China—under any circumstances. In view of the American ability to read Japanese diplomatic traffic, a warning of imminent war was thereupon sent out from Washington.

Since neither the German nor the Italian governments had developed a reputation for adhering to their promises, whether or not in treaty form, the Tokyo government checked a few days before actually striking whether the promise to go to war with the United States still held. Positive answers were received promptly. Hitler in fact had been seriously worried that the growing troubles experienced by the Germans on the Eastern front might discourage Japan from striking, and he repeatedly made and authorized far more positive announcements about the situation there than reality warranted. Between Roosevelt's hopes of delaying the Japanese until they could see that Germany was not as certain to win the war as they believed and Hitler's concern lest exactly that realization might occur to the Japanese and discourage them from this attack, it was the German leader's hope that won, by a margin of two weeks—Japan struck before the German defeat outside Moscow became obvious.

The Japanese advance

Japan's war plan called for a series of prompt moves to occupy Thailand and invade Malaya, to invade the Philippines, to seize the American held islands of Guam and Wake, and then to conquer the Dutch East Indies, Burma, and the British, American, and French held islands in the South Pacific. These moves needed to be shielded from American and British naval interference. The Japanese navy's previous plan to meet an American fleet moving to protect and/or rescue the Philippines in a major naval battle in the western Pacific was abandoned in mid-October 1941 in favour of Admiral Yamamoto Isoroku's project of a peacetime carrier-plane attack on American warships in Pearl Harbor. This was because Admiral Yamamoto Isoroku threatened to resign as commander of the combined fleet unless his plan was adopted. The 7 December 1941 attack had a devastating impact on the American navy and thus did remove it from threatening the flank of the Japanese push south. It also, however, had much wider negative effects for Japan's prospects in the overall war, effects that could have been easily predicted.

The unprovoked attack on a Sunday in peacetime—which enthused Hitler, who had done this to Yugoslavia in April of that year—aroused a violent reaction from the American public, nullifying all Japanese hopes for an eventual negotiated settlement of the conflict. The Japanese had assumed that the Americans would never choose to expend blood and treasure to reconquer islands they had never heard of, and so these could be returned to the colonial masters of whom they disapproved. However, the reality was exactly the opposite: the Americans were now prepared to fight until Japan was crushed. In that fight, they would be assisted by two other predictable features of the attack on Pearl Harbor. In view of the shallow water of the base—something the Japanese had known about and so had utilized special shallow moving torpedoes—all but two of the eight American battleships the Japanese imagined they had sunk had in fact simply settled into the mud from where they could be raised and repaired, and subsequently returned to service. As for the crews, although the loss of life on the *Arizona* was great and substantial numbers were killed or wounded on the other warships hit, the overwhelming majority of the trained and experienced crew members of ships that had been in port in peace on a Sunday survived the attack. The extraordinarily rapid revival of the American navy was due not only to the arrival of new warships built in the country's yards but also to the availability of thousands of seamen from the ships that had been struck.

The two British warships sent to Singapore in the hope of deterring Japan arrived in early December and left harbour on news of the Japanese landing in northern Malaya. These warships were located by a Japanese submarine, and they were attacked by Japanese planes with torpedoes and bombs. In the absence of any British air cover or effective anti-aircraft armament, both were sunk on 10 December. There was very little British air force available due to the pressing need for cover within the United Kingdom and the Mediterranean. The Japanese force that had landed on the coast was able to push inland relatively quickly. The defending British ground force consisted of two Indian and one Australian division together with minimal units from Britain. The three Japanese divisions commanded by General Yamashita Tomoyuki had begun landing on 8 December and pushed south against faltering resistance. The British sent additional troops to bolster the defence, but while there was hard fighting in a few places, the Japanese drove the 300 miles to the southern end of Malaya by the beginning of February. The crossing of Japanese forces to the island of Singapore, beginning during the night of 8–9 February, led, after some fighting, to a British surrender on 15 February, with an army substantially larger than the attacking Japanese force headed for captivity. In Singapore itself, Japanese soldiers murdered and raped civilians by the thousands. There were incidents of horror wherever the Japanese army operated; but a

71

similar incident of mass violence occurred only once more—in Manila in March 1945, with Yamashita again in command.

When British forces at Singapore surrendered, the Japanese had seized the British colony of Hong Kong as well as the American island of Guam, and, after an earlier failed attempt, they also took Wake Island. They were, however, still embroiled in bitter fighting on Luzon in the Philippines, where President Roosevelt had sent General MacArthur to assist in the development of a Philippine army capable of defending the country when independence had been scheduled for 1944. MacArthur had reversed the earlier defence plan, which had focused on holding the Bataan Peninsula to deny Japan the use of Manila harbour, in favour of an unrealistic plan to defend the whole island of Luzon. The Japanese plan provided for an attack on the American air force on 8 December, and landings both in the north of Luzon and south of Manila on 10 December. The air strike, though some ten hours after the attack on Pearl Harbor, caught most of MacArthur's planes on the ground, and both landings succeeded. It quickly became apparent that the new defence plan was not working, and surviving American and Philippine units moved to Bataan. The needed food and other supplies had not been stapled there because of the changed plan, which meant that the American and Philippine soldiers were weakened terribly by hunger and disease. They nevertheless put up a far harder fight than the Japanese had expected. The Japanese commander, General Homma Masaharu, had to obtain reinforcements. The exhausted defenders were driven back and had to surrender on 8 April with the fortress island of Corregidor surrendering on 6 May and the remaining defenders in the Philippines surrendering on 9 June. Thousands of the soldiers who had surrendered on Bataan were murdered by the Japanese military as they were driven to camps. The survivors were systematically exploited and often murdered in prisoner of war camps and mines. Roosevelt had earlier ordered MacArthur to leave Bataan for Australia to command American forces that were to be sent there. In the

Philippines, there developed both substantial collaboration with the Japanese and a small but growing resistance and guerrilla movement. The latter provided some trouble for the Japanese and intelligence for the Americans.

Japanese conquests of Malaya and the Philippines were preliminary to their intended conquest of the Dutch East Indies. Already on 15 December Japanese forces landed on the island of Borneo, which was then partly under British and partly under Dutch control. In the following weeks the Japanese landed on one island in the area after another. They destroyed a combined Dutch, American, and British fleet in the Naval Battle of the Java Sea at the end of February and forced the surrender of the largest Allied force in the area, on Java, on 8 March. By then they had also landed both at the western, Dutch, portion of the huge island of New Guinea and on its northeastern coast, where they seized the towns of Lae and Salamaua. Japanese expeditions from the Mariana and Caroline islands mandated to them after World War I headed for the islands to the south and quite rapidly took over the Admiralty, Gilbert, and Bismarck islands as well as most of the Solomon Islands (Map 7 and 8). Of special importance was that their seizure of the Bismarck island group included the major port of Rabaul at the northern end of New Britain. It became the central base for the Japanese campaign that now threatened Australia and New Zealand.

Simultaneously with this conquest of the Dutch East Indies and large numbers of British territories and islands in the South Pacific, the Japanese army drove into Burma. On the same date that Java surrendered, the Japanese entered Rangoon. In subsequent weeks, they drove the British, Chinese, and a small American force out of the rest of Burma, attaining essentially complete control by the end of April. This conquest, and the occupation of islands in the Indian Ocean, raised the possibility, welcome to Vichy, of a Japanese occupation of the island of Madagascar, thereby closing off the Allied sea supply route to

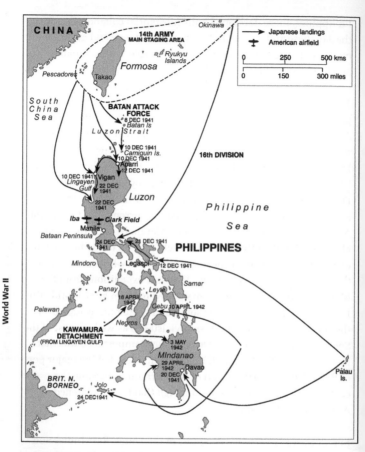

7. The Philippines 1941–42

India, to the Middle East, and to the Soviet Union across Iran. In view of this danger, British forces with indirect American support landed at the northern end of Madagascar on 4 May 1942, and in subsequent months took the whole island. The Japanese had not only missed an opportunity there but because of differences between the army and navy, they had also refrained for the time

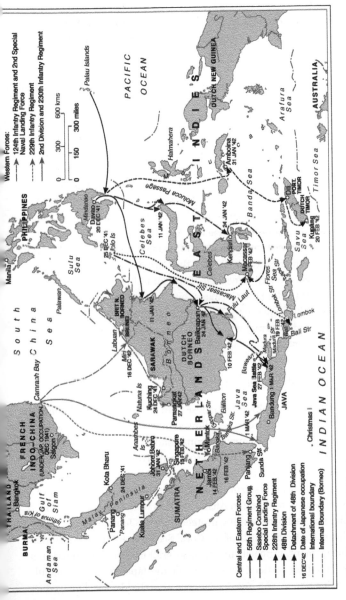

Western Forces:

→ 124th Infantry Regiment and 2nd Special Naval Landing Force
→ 229th Infantry Regiment
→ 2nd Division and 230th Infantry Regiment

Central and Eastern Forces:

→ 56th Regiment Group
→ Sasebo Combined Special Landing Force
→ 228th Infantry Regiment
→ 48th Division
→ Detachment of 48th Division
16 DEC '42 Date of Japanese occupation
---- International boundary
---- Internal boundary (Borneo)

8. The East Indies 1941–42

75

being from invading India or landing on Ceylon (Sri Lanka). They had, however, worked out a division of Asia with the Germans.

In December Tokyo formally proposed to Berlin a division of Asia at the 70th degree longitude. This would give Japan most of Siberia, all of China, most of India, and all of southeast Asia. While some in the German high command wanted more of the Siberian industrial area, Hitler accepted the proposal, and an agreement was signed in February. In the office of Tojo Hideki, prime minister as well as war minister since October 1941, a project was developed in December for the division of the South Pacific and the Western hemisphere. It provided for Japan to acquire all islands in the Pacific, Australia and New Zealand, Alaska, the western provinces of Canada, the state of Washington, Central America, the islands in the Caribbean, Ecuador, Columbia, western Venezuela, Peru, and Chile. This proposal was not placed before the Germans, but since it left the majority of the Western hemisphere to Germany, it is unlikely that Hitler, who had agreed for a majority of Asia to go to Japan, would have found it objectionable.

Japan's offensives halted

Before these ambitious Japanese plans could be realized, the early victories would have to be followed by many more. There was division within the Japanese command structure as to where to go next, and this had already led to the abortion of further advances into India and the Indian Ocean. A substantial further move south would require the seizure of Port Moresby on the south coast of New Guinea to threaten Australia. This was attempted with a planned seaborne landing protected by the Japanese navy. This thrust led to the Battle of the Coral Sea on 3–8 May 1942. In that engagement, primarily involving aircraft carriers, the Americans lost the fleet carrier *Lexington* while the Japanese lost the small carrier 'Shoho' and one fleet carrier of each side was damaged.

Whatever the relative losses, the strategic victory was with the Americans because the Japanese abandoned the landing assault on Port Moresby. They would instead move to take that town by an overland move across New Guinea on the Kokoda Trail but were stopped short of their goal by Australian forces, aided by American air units, on 17 September 1942. By that date, the Japanese attempt to seize a combined Australian–American base at Milne Bay at the southeastern end of New Guinea had also been crushed.

Immediately after the setback at Coral Sea, the Japanese decided on two further operations. They would bomb the American air and naval base at Dutch Harbor and seize the two western islands Kiska and Attu in the Aleutian chain off the coast of Alaska. Two carriers sent planes to bomb Dutch Harbor and then escorted the landing detachments that took the two islands in early June 1942. Although this operation might provide a base for further conquests in that area as well as prevent American attacks on Japan from that direction, the carriers involved could not participate in the major naval action occurring simultaneously further south. That was the Japanese operation to seize the island of Midway on which Yamamoto had again obtained his way by threatening to resign as commander of the combined fleet. It is possible that there was also greater willingness in the Japanese command structure to approve this operation because of the air raid by American planes led by Colonel James Doolittle on Tokyo on 18 April 1942.

While the Americans had the carrier *Yorktown*, which had been damaged at Coral Sea, at least partially repaired at Pearl Harbor, neither the Japanese fleet carrier damaged at Coral Sea nor the one that had lost many of its planes in that battle was included in the force that was to destroy the rest of the American navy in the Hawaii area and seize the island of Midway. An additional two of the six carriers in the Japanese fleet headed for Midway were held back to protect the fleet of battleships and cruisers that was expected to destroy the American fleet when it sallied to protect Midway. However, American intelligence officers at Hawaii had puzzled out the Japanese plan, and the American navy's three carriers were ready to surprise the four Japanese carriers southeast of Midway on 4 June. As the Japanese shot down low flying American torpedo planes, the American dive bombers sank three of the Japanese carriers and, soon after, the fourth carrier. The *Yorktown* was seriously damaged and then sunk by a Japanese submarine, but the battle clearly favoured the Americans. The Japanese battle fleet turned back, having lost a cruiser and some other warships, but more importantly the Americans could and did replace the carrier that had been lost and the aircrew that had been killed while the Japanese could not replace the carriers. Furthermore, the Japanese had never established a serious programme of training aircrew replacements, so that the loss of experienced pilots at Coral Sea and Midway meant that, thereafter, the Japanese would always face a shortage of well trained pilots.

The Battle of Midway halted Japanese advances in the Pacific and opened the way for an American counter-offensive. That came in August 1942 at Guadalcanal and will be covered in Chapter 6. What is critical for an understanding of the war in general is that the Japanese advance, though halted, had obliged the United States to depart temporarily from its 'Europe First' strategy and instead send a majority of its newly mobilized and available forces to the Pacific theatre throughout 1942 and into the first months of 1943. This process delayed American operations in the Mediterranean and European theatres. However, the Axis powers were unable to take advantage of this delay because of their own failure to coordinate operations. This failure is summed up by the fact that the Germans only learned that Japan had lost, not won, the Battles of Coral Sea and Midway when the Japanese asked to purchase the uncompleted German aircraft carrier *Graf Zeppelin* and haul it to the Pacific. Presumably the Americans, who decoded the relevant messages, were disappointed that Germany turned down this request.

A wider war

As soon as Hitler heard of the Japanese attack on Pearl Harbor, he ordered the German navy to go to war with the United States and eight other countries in the Western hemisphere. He did not want to wait the three or four days needed to summon the German parliament, give them the good news of war with the United States, and go through the diplomatic formalities. Italy also promptly declared war on the United States. So did three other states aligned with Germany: Hungary, Romania, and Bulgaria. While President Roosevelt sent messages to Congress for declarations of war against Japan, Germany, and Italy, which Congress promptly passed, he had the State Department try for six months to get the other three countries to withdraw their declarations. When they absolutely refused to do this, he gave up negotiations in June 1942, and Congress accommodated the aggressors by declaring war in turn. Whatever the intentions of the leaders of Hungary, Romania, and Bulgaria, in alliance with Germany, with regards to the United States, there was no question about the immediate threat from Germany and Italy: it was from submarines in the Atlantic and Caribbean.

In anticipation of war with the United States, Admiral Dönitz, the commander of German submarines, had sent a number of these towards the American east coast. In the first six months of 1942 they sank many Allied merchant ships as no convoy system was in effect and the coast was not blacked out. German submarines surfaced at night and torpedoed ships silhouetted against the lights of hotels, motels, and houses. The German effort was also assisted by a change in their navy's code system that interrupted Allied ability to decipher naval radio messages for much of 1942. As if this setback for the American navy was not enough, there was what must be called a disaster for the country's own submarines. It turned out that the torpedoes provided to them were hopelessly defective. At the beginning of the war, the German navy had encountered a somewhat similar problem, but it had been corrected much more rapidly than the Americans' problem. Not until well into 1943 could American submarine commanders and crews rely on the torpedoes they fired at Japanese ships to run at the depth they were supposed to and to explode when they hit. The extreme vulnerability of Japanese navy and industry to being deprived of oil and other materials could not be exploited until well into the conflict.

The war now included all major powers, and at a conference in Washington in January 1942, the Allies called themselves the United Nations, a label under which they would fight together and later organize a new world organization. Nothing similar ever appeared on the other side.

Chapter 6
The turning tide:
autumn 1942–spring 1944

Germany's 1942 offensive and disaster in the East

After the Germans had essentially stabilized the Eastern front in April–May 1942, they initiated 'Operation Blue', their offensive for that year. The losses they had suffered the preceding year precluded a repetition of offensives on the whole front. There would be only one on the southern portion to seize the Caucasus oilfields, thus simultaneously depriving the Soviets of this essential resource and enriching the Axis war effort. Any success of this offensive would involve lengthening the flanks of the advance, so in the winter of 1941–2 the Germans urged their Romanian, Italian, and Hungarian allies to increase their commitment of troops to the Eastern front, which they did. The Germans, however, did not provide their allies with the needed anti-tank guns and other modern equipment and would be surprised when, in the winter of 1942–3, Red Army offensives sliced through the parts of the front these units held.

On the southern segment of the front, the Soviets had made some significant gains in their winter offensives, but most were undone by German operations before they launched Operation Blue on 28 June. Many Red Army reserves had been held before Moscow in mistaken anticipation of a German offensive there, and so initially German forces advanced substantially. Two developments affected the development of the fighting. For the first time, Stalin allowed front commanders to arrange substantial retreats, so that German encirclement drives failed to bring in the huge numbers of captives characteristic of 1941. Second, the Germans not only sent an army group towards the Caucasus through a retaken Rostov but had another army group drive towards the Volga at Stalingrad to protect the northern flank of their expected conquest. Both thrusts first advanced substantially but were slowed and then halted. On the one hand, the Germans had not been able to replace fully the human and material losses suffered the preceding year, while on the other hand Red Army units fought bitterly and increasingly ably. In the southern thrust, the Germans captured the Maikop oilfield but were halted both before Novorossisk on the Black Sea coast and before Grozhny in the Caucasus at the end of August. At the same time, the German force headed for Stalingrad had reached the Volga but was stopped in and around that city (Map 9).

The Germans bombed Stalingrad heavily and fought their way into the city as the Red Army contested every block and counter-attacked repeatedly, especially on the northern sector of the urban front. More and more German units were thrown into street fighting while the Soviets sent reinforcements into the city across the Volga. Since the two German army groups were 200 miles apart, they could not assist each other as both tried to grind forward. The Red Army launched first a minor and then a major offensive on the front before Moscow, but both failed to dislodge the Germans from positions they had held the preceding winter. However, the situation at Stalingrad was different.

The flanks of the German advance into Stalingrad were held primarily by Romanian armies assisted by some German units. As the Stavka, the Red Army command, dribbled reinforcements into Stalingrad, it prepared massive offensives against the northern and southern flanks of the Germans fighting within the city. Having waited until the Western Allies landed in northwest

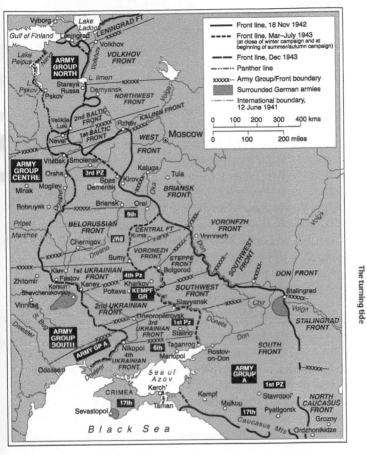

9. German–Soviet War 1942–43

Africa, which thereby tied down German forces in the West
(a subject reviewed subsequently), the Red Army launched
'Operation Uranus' on 19 November. Both in the north and the
south, massive armoured units and infantry broke through
defending Romanian and German forces, meeting a few days
later. Even before the formal junction, Hitler had both created a
new army group that was to break through the developing

83

encirclement and ordered General, soon promoted to Field Marshal Friedrich Paulus to stand fast in the city. The German air force was to provide supplies to the German 6th Army and attached units in the pocket and the new army group was to break the encirclement. That offensive started on 12 December but failed. Subsequently the Red Army both battered the encircled Germans and crushed the Italian army holding a portion of the front northwest of Stalingrad. The last German survivors in the ruins of the city surrendered at the end of January 1943. Critically, the fighting and German defeat at Stalingrad dominated the world's headlines for months and looked to many on both sides like a major turning point in the war. In practical terms it also obliged the Germans to pull back the army group that had advanced into the Caucasus lest it too be cut off. That force held onto a portion of the land taken earlier, the Kuban bridgehead, from which Hitler hoped to strike into the Caucasus again in 1943. However, this plan proved impossible for a now weakened Germany, and the area was evacuated in early October 1943.

The collapse of the German southern front tempted the Soviets to push more rapidly than the situation warranted; and in late February 1943 the Germans struck into the advancing Red Army units, retook Kharkov, and showed the Soviet leadership that in spite of their victory at Stalingrad, much difficult fighting still lay ahead. Perhaps it was this experience that led Stalin to heed the advice of his military commanders to go on the defensive, await the 1943 German summer offensive, and only then move to major offensives. The bulge around the city of Kursk looked to both sides the obvious site of the next major encounter: the Soviets turned it into the most heavily fortified area yet, and the Germans prepared to assault it from both north and south (Map 10). The German offensive was repeatedly postponed as the Germans resupplied their forces, especially with the new heavy tanks, the Mark V Panther and Mark VI Tiger, which had been ordered and designed after they had learned in 1941 that the Red Army had the bigger and better tanks.

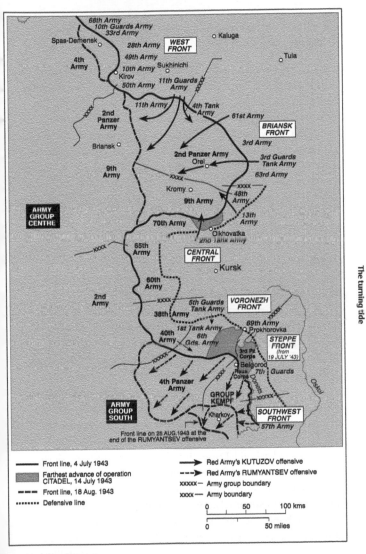

Front line, 4 July 1943

Farthest advance of operation CITADEL, 14 July 1943

Front line, 18 Aug. 1943

Defensive line

Red Army's KUTUZOV offensive

Red Army's RUMYANTSEV offensive

xxxxx — Army group boundary

xxxx — Army boundary

```
0          50          100 kms
0              50 miles
```

10. Battle of Kursk

The initiative in the East and shifts in the Mediterranean in 1943

On 5 July the Germans launched Operation Citadel to crush Soviet forces in the Kursk bulge and regain the initiative in the east. After several days of bitter fighting at both segments of the front, the Germans battered their way forward and inflicted very heavy losses on the Red Army, but they still failed to break through. Although the loss statistics favoured the Germans, the reality was that the Germans could not afford their losses, and their inability to make a significant breakthrough implied a major failure. The ending of the offensive was speeded up by news of the landing by the Western Allies in Sicily as well as a Soviet offensive into the Orel area behind the northern German attack into the Kursk bulge. From here on the Red Army had the initiative and took it at a time when the Red Army's air force was gaining control of the air over a battlefield where the German air force—facing demands in the Mediterranean and at home—was stretched ever thinner.

A series of major Soviet offensives first drove back the German army on the central part of the front, then pushed into the Ukraine, and at the end of the year broke the siege of Leningrad. In these offensives, the Red Army showed that its officers had learned a great deal, while the German armed forces were clearly weakening. Even if the lead in the quality of tanks had shifted somewhat against them, the Red Army had so many more tanks, most produced in its factories and some provided by the Americans under Lend-Lease, that there was no way the Germans could block determined Soviet offensives. These were invariably supported by the employment of artillery on a stupendous scale and enjoyed two major advantages in the later years of the war. On the one hand, the partisan movement interfered with German communications and transportation when ordered to do so at critical times and places. On the other hand, German intelligence on the Eastern front, headed by General Reinhard Gehlen from early 1942 on, was almost invariably fooled by Soviet disinformation and Gehlen's hopeless incompetence. The spring of 1944 saw the Soviets in a position to decide how best to crush the remaining German forces in the Soviet Union, and they coordinated their timing with their allies.

The Western Allies were fighting a multi-front war, unlike the Soviets who could concentrate on just one. Having finally held the German–Italian advance in Egypt in July 1942, the British with American support prepared an offensive there. It started at the end of October: in a grinding battle at El Alamein they defeated the Axis force, pushed its remnants slowly through the Egyptian and Libyan deserts, and were to be met by a combined American and British landing in French northwest Africa. Those landings, called 'Operation Torch', succeeded in getting ashore on both the Atlantic and Mediterranean coasts of Morocco and Algeria on 8 November. The Vichy units at first fought against the landings, but then General Dwight Eisenhower, the Allied commander, made an arrangement with the Vichy leader, Admiral François Darlan, who was there because of his son's illness, to end the fighting and have some French troops now under his command switch sides. Because the Vichy-loyal commander in Tunisia offered no resistance to German and Italian forces quickly thrown across the Mediterranean from Sicily, the Axis powers could hold the key places in Tunisia, Tunis, and Bizerte and stop the advancing Allied armies. These events have to be seen in the wider context of war. Hitler had hoped to drive the Allies out of northwest Africa, but he could not send enough forces there because of the Soviet offensive at Stalingrad. On the other hand, the German army sent to Tunisia could not be employed in the effort to break the Stalingrad encirclement. The critical impact for the Western Allies was that the need for a campaign to seize Tunisia from the Axis forces there, who were joined by those retreating from El Alamein, meant that there would not thereafter be sufficient time in 1943 to move troops from Africa to Britain for an invasion across the Channel in that year; it had to be postponed to 1944.

During the fighting in Tunisia, American and British political and military leaders met at Casablanca in January to plan future steps. It was clear that there could not be an invasion of France in 1943, and to make a real contribution to the fight against the Axis that year, it was decided to invade Sicily as soon as possible after victory in Tunisia, and thereafter perhaps mainland Italy. The air offensive against Germany would proceed on an increasing scale with the American air force concentrating on efforts to hit industrial and other important targets by day while the Royal Air Force would continue to concentrate on bombing cities by night. Because of the steady monthly losses of ships at a greater rate than the Allies could build them, the fight against Germany's submarines was allocated the highest priority in 1943. Both to calm down the upsets caused in Britain and the United States by the deal with Darlan and to reassure the Soviets that postponement of the invasion in the West did not mean any relaxation of the war effort of the Western Allies, this was also the occasion for public announcement of a policy both had arrived at long before: the countries of the Axis would have to surrender unconditionally. The suggestion to exempt Italy had been vetoed by the London cabinet, and Roosevelt and Churchill devised a way to make the announcement a special part of their public message from Casablanca.

By the time of the Casablanca Conference, Darlan had been assassinated by a French royalist, and the two Allied leaders had tried to reconcile the Free French leader de Gaulle with the French general Henri Giraud who had escaped from a German prison camp. De Gaulle had soon pushed Giraud aside and established a provisional French government at Algiers. Substantial numbers of French troops in north Africa joined the larger British and American forces that fought in Tunisia against the Axis units now trapped between them and the British force that had driven across Libya. At Kasserine Pass near the southern end of the Tunisian front a German strike defeated a part of the untried American army, but the Germans were halted, and in the subsequent months they were driven into the northeastern corner of Tunisia where well over 270,000 Axis soldiers surrendered in early May 1943. Just as German transport planes trying to supply the encircled German army in Stalingrad could not fly to supply Axis units in Tunisia, so the planes that did fly from Sicily to Tunisia could not augment the air supply of the Stalingrad pocket. Similarly, the Americans had been obliged to divert forces to the Pacific by the Japanese advance, and the European Axis was also being obliged to engage several fronts simultaneously.

The war at sea and in the air

The operations following the Axis surrender in Tunisia, and the landings on Sicily and the Italian mainland, presupposed an Allied turning of the tide in the war at sea, which they had made their highest priority. In spite of difficult convoy battles with German submarines in March and April, the Allies attained a major victory in May and June of 1943. The employment of more long-range planes, escort carriers, ship-borne radar, additional escort warships, and renewed breaks into the German naval code enabled the British, American, and Canadian navies to sink so many German submarines that Dönitz gave up on the North Atlantic. He received encouragement from Hitler for the development of two new classes of submarines, and the German leader would subordinate strategy on the northern portion of the Eastern front to the need to control the Baltic Sea so that these new submarines and their crews could be tried and trained. However, by the time these were ready, in April 1945, the war was ending. The Allies, on the other hand, had removed the stranglehold that shipping losses had placed on their strategic choices when new building had exceeded total losses in the autumn of 1943 and continued to do so ever more thereafter.

Both the British and the Americans substantially increased their air attacks on Germany and German held parts of Europe during 1942 and 1943. The major British raids on Hamburg in July 1943 touched off for the first time a firestorm—a type of urban disaster that recurred several times in later raids. Whatever the arguments then and after the war about the effectiveness of the strategic bombing offensive and the morality of targeting cities, several aspects of these operations are beyond doubt. The German people, who had been so enthusiastic about the Nazi regime's breaking the restrictions imposed by the 1919 peace treaty, were now experiencing what the victors of World War I had attempted to prevent. After 1945 some German cities have deliberately maintained a major ruined building, usually a church, to remind succeeding generations of what can happen. Another significant impact of bombing was that there was considerable disruption of industrial production, the transportation system, and the critical synthetic oil industry. By 1943 the Germans were firing more shells into the air than across the fronts, and by 1944 there was more German artillery aimed at the sky than at ground targets. In addition literally hundreds of thousands of men, prisoners, and eventually male and female youngsters were used to operate the anti-aircraft system. Just as the 1,000 submarines Germany built during the war utilized materials that could otherwise have enabled the production of about 30,000 tanks for the Eastern front, so the diversion of German resources to coping with the bombing campaign assisted the Soviets, who were doing most of the fighting.

This diversion of German resources to the defence against bombing threatened to turn the tide in the air war against the Western Allies in the autumn of 1943. The combination of large numbers of German fighters with ground-based anti-aircraft fire inflicted increasing losses on the attacking bombers. With the loss ratio rising to high levels, the Allies had to change their operations because complete control of the air over Western Europe was as much a prerequisite for any invasion there as it had been for the Germans for any invasion of England. It was in this context that the need to escort bombers all the way to their targets by fighters led to the successful role of the F-51 Mustang fighter and major air battles in February and March of 1944. The subsequent development of the war in Europe was greatly affected by, first, the failure of the Germans to reverse their defeat at sea in June 1943; and, second, the success of the Allies in reversing the problems that their air forces had faced in the autumn of that year.

Campaigns in Sicily and Italy

The immediate follow-up to the Tunisian campaign was the landing of British and American forces on Sicily in 'Operation Husky' on 10 July 1943. The landings from the sea were preceded by a deception that led the Germans to expect invasions elsewhere and airborne assaults that involved massive confusion on the Allied side but did assist the landings a little. Italian units dissolved relatively quickly while the German units fought hard, at one point threatening to crush the American landing at Gela. As the British 8th Army, ran into difficulties in the southeast corner of the island, its commander, General Montgomery, had the unit take over one of the main routes assigned by planners to the American 7th Army, with the result that General Patton headed it towards Palermo in the northwest corner. That push worked, but then the Allies had to drive the Germans out of the northeastern part of the island, something they succeeded in doing, but only with the bulk of German forces escaping across the Strait of Messina (Map 11).

The Allied conquest of Sicily had three major effects on the war. It helped precipitate the fall of Mussolini, who was dismissed by his fascist associates on 25 July and then arrested by order of King Victor Emanuel. Fascism had lost its support in the Italian population as the regime had lost the country's colonial empire; had suffered a great number of casualties on an Eastern front that Italians had had no interest in having their country committed to; and, it must be added, had fully aligned the country with the Germans, who were generally disliked by Italians, especially as

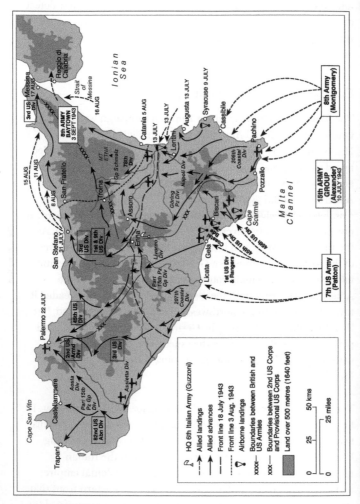

11. Sicilian campaign

German troops now poured into the country at Hitler's orders. This last point is related to the second result of the Sicilian campaign. As it became obvious to the German high command that the Italian military and public were tired of the war, they realized that German troops would have to replace Italian units stationed in occupied France, Yugoslavia, and Greece as well as in the defence of Italy itself. This realization had been particularly brought home by the Italian surrender of September 1943, but it had begun months before.

The third result of Allied victory on Sicily was interrelated with the second: the Allies decided to invade the mainland of Italy while the successor Italian government of Pietro Badoglio was negotiating a surrender. Allied landings in September, with the British landing at the toe of Italy and a combined American-British force landing at Salerno near Naples, obliged the Germans to choose between committing substantial forces to the defense of Italy or simply abandoning it. They decided on the former, so that henceforth two whole German armies were committed to the fighting there, unable either to shore up the retreating German army on the Eastern front or to reinforce German forces in France and Belgium needed to ward off any Allied landing there.

The fighting in Italy pitted two Allied armies against two German ones, with Allied control of the air off-setting the terrain which favoured the defence. In bitter fighting, the Allies pushed up the peninsula. While the effort to break what looked like a slowly moving deadlock by a landing on the coast south of Rome at Anzio in January 1944 did not have the desired result, the Allies did seize the Foggia peninsula, which provided, as anticipated, airfields from which bombers could reach important targets in German controlled or allied parts of central and southeastern Europe. Just as the Soviets planned for a big push in the summer of 1944, so the Western Allies anticipated launching a major new offensive in Italy at about the same time.

The war in the Pacific 1942–43

In the months when the Allies were halting and then pushing back the Axis powers in north Africa and Europe, they were engaged in very similar operations in the Pacific and east Asia. After their major defensive naval victory at Midway, the Americans in early August 1942 launched an offensive into the Solomon Islands where the construction of a Japanese airfield on Guadalcanal threatened American sea communications with Australia. The Japanese adopted by choice the procedure that the situation of their just developing substantial forces obliged the Americans to follow: dribbling in reinforcements. The result was a six-months-long battle of attrition that the Americans won; the Japanese evacuated the remnant of their units on Guadalcanal in February 1943. While the Americans could replace their losses and actually increased their forces in the Pacific, the Japanese were in no position to do so. As the battles on, over, and around Guadalcanal went forward, the American and Australian forces on New Guinea were pushing the Japanese back across the Kokoda trail and then carried out a series of landings on the island's northern coast.

The Americans now looked to a strategy of defeating Japan by a double thrust in the Pacific aided by two additional offensives in east Asia. In the southwest Pacific a series of landing operations led by General Douglas MacArthur would move through the islands the Japanese had occupied in their initial offensive until the Philippines were reached as a basis for the attack on the Japanese home islands. In the Central Pacific, naval operations with marines and army units under Admiral Chester Nimitz would, after reclaiming the two Aleutian islands the Japanese had seized, strike through the island groups that the Japanese had seized from the British and the ones mandated to them after the prior war, head for either the Philippines or Taiwan, and then strike at Japan. It was hoped that a third offensive could be launched from China, which was much closer to the Japanese home islands, and that a Soviet assault from the north after victory over Germany would keep Japanese forces in China busy and threaten the home islands from an additional direction.

As fighting had been under way in China since 1937, it may be helpful to turn to that theatre now. The Japanese army in China periodically launched local offensives into areas still under the control of the Nationalist government, but the latter continued to fight back. The United States supported a small unit of fighter planes in China and hoped to add bombers that could reach the Japanese home islands. The efforts to work with the British to clear northern Burma of the Japanese had as a major purpose not only increasing supplies to the Nationalists but also to make possible the deployment of bombers. Until a new connecting road could be built or the original one cut by the Japanese reopened, an airlift operation across the Himalayas from the Assam province of northeast India, called 'The Hump', delivered some supplies.

Three elements combined to lead the Japanese to launch two major offensives in the summer of 1944. The development of air bases in China from which American long-range bombers could reach Japan, the increase in the air supply route from Assam, and the increasing successes of Allied submarines in sinking Japanese shipping led to the decision to launch the 'Ichigo' offensive in China to seize the new airfields and simultaneously open a railway connection into the Japanese holdings in southeast Asia, now isolated by the Allied sinking of many Japanese merchant ships. Furthermore, a major offensive into Assam from Burma would cut the air supply route and might also produce an uprising in India. The offensive in China was entirely successful. In the long run, it helped pave the way for the communist victory there in the later civil war; in the short run it effectively ended both the bombing of Japan from China and the thought of an invasion of the home islands from China. The invasion of India's Assam province ended in the Japanese army's greatest defeat of the war as the British–Indian army crushed them in the battle of Imphal-Kohima and thereafter initiated the clearing out of the Japanese from central and southern Burma.

In the southwest Pacific, American forces with some Australian assistance pushed back the Japanese with a series of landings in the Solomon and Admiralty islands, and on the north coast of New Guinea. By the summer of 1944, these had reached a point where the remaining Japanese holdings and bases were effectively isolated as the Americans prepared for an assault on the Philippines. In the central Pacific theatre, another series of landings, starting with one on Tarawa in the Gilbert Islands, had moved towards the Marianas, where the first landing, that on Saipan, took place in June 1944. On this route also Japanese forces and bases were left behind and its navy decimated. The submarine campaign against Japanese shipping—now effective because of breaks into Japanese codes and the use of torpedoes that worked—made it increasingly difficult for Japan to draw on the resources of lands seized in the winter of 1941–2.

Resistance in occupied areas and the policies of neutrals as the tide turns

The clear signs in all theatres of war that the Allies had turned the war around served to encourage resistance movements in territories that the Germans, Italians, and Japanese had occupied earlier and were still holding. This was true in Western and Southeastern Europe as well as in Denmark and Norway. There, as in the Philippines, Dutch East Indies, and other areas still held by the Japanese, the horrendous conduct of the occupation forces contributed to increasing resistance. The Allies often had contact with the resistance movements and provided them with weapons. The shift by the British government regarding the situation in Yugoslavia from supporting the royalist Chetniks to supporting the communist partisans contributed to the victory of the latter in the civil war and to the postwar move to independence from the Soviet Union by their leader Tito.

The obvious shift in the war also affected the conduct of those few countries that were still neutral. Turkey reduced chrome deliveries to Germany and declared war on it in February 1945. Portugal objected less vehemently to Allied use of the Azores in the Battle of the Atlantic, and Spain reduced its forces fighting alongside Germany on the Eastern front. Sweden slowly shifted from assisting Germany, and only Switzerland continued to help the Germans economically into the last weeks of the war.

An important factor in the shift of the war was the willingness of the Allies to at least try to coordinate their efforts. At conferences and by diplomatic and military missions, they did this even though there were frequent arguments and differences. Conferences in Moscow, Cairo, and Teheran in 1943 symbolized this procedure publicly, but the Americans and British in particular learned to work together effectively. The Germans, Italians, and Japanese, on the other hand, never tried to coordinate strategy or to keep one another informed. While the Allies at times even shared secret intelligence, the Axis powers did nothing of the sort.

Chapter 7

Developments on the home front and in technical and medical fields

Germany

The impact of the war on the home fronts of the aggressors was dramatic. Rationing began in Germany in late August 1939. For much of the war, rations in Germany were the highest in Europe, and in the first years were supplemented by millions of packages sent home by soldiers from lands occupied by the German army. These packages included both goods stolen in huge quantities and those bought with deliberately undervalued currencies. This situation deteriorated in the years of 1943–5 as the German army retreated and Allied bombing disrupted the transportation system. A substantial part of Germany's housing was destroyed or damaged by bombing and, in the last seven months, by fighting inside the country. There was also less clothing, furniture, and other items stolen from murdered Jews and those in the occupied countries to distribute to bombed out Germans by the National Socialist Welfare Organization. On the other hand, top Nazis, Hitler, Göring, and Alfred Rosenberg, devoted much time and effort to looting art all over Europe.

The programmes of compulsory sterilization of those thought likely to have defective offspring and special awards and medals for those having the 'right' kind of children in large numbers that had been instituted in 1933 continued without serious objections into the last weeks of the war. The project initiated in 1939 to kill all the seriously disabled, mentally and physically, and others in nursing homes and old folks' homes drew some objections from the Christian churches. Since the victims had relatives in the 'Aryan' populations, the regime, whose leaders believed Germany had not been defeated in World War I but had been stabbed in the back by troubles at home, changed the procedure to calm the uproar. In August 1941, the killing was officially ordered to stop, but in reality it continued in a decentralized manner until occupation authorities forcibly halted it. The process of decentralized killing freed those active in the centres where people had been murdered for transfer to new institutions in occupied Poland created for the systematic killing of Jews.

Germany was covered by camps and sub-camps in which prisoners of war, kidnapped slave labourers, and any thought to be opposed to the regime were held and from which they were, literally by the millions, taken to work alongside Germans who had not been drafted. German society was affected by the continuation of the police system established earlier and the universal knowledge of it and by fear of denunciation. Despite over five million German soldiers and several hundred thousand civilians having been killed, the vast majority of Germans supported the regime up until the last weeks of the war.

Poland

No country was more dramatically changed by the war than Poland. It was divided in 1939 between Germany and the Soviet Union; then the Germans occupied the part allocated to the Soviets; then the Red Army occupied the whole country; and, finally, Poland was moved westwards, yielding its eastern parts to the Soviet Union and acquiring formerly German lands in the west and north. Both the Germans and the Soviets killed large numbers and deported many of the Polish people, but there were basic differences in their policies. The Germans had decided to kill all Jews worldwide, which meant over three million Polish Jews were murdered with only a tiny remnant surviving in hiding or after deportation. The Soviets, on the other hand, simply deported a disproportionately large number of Jews, many of whom died in the process—but because the survivors had been deported to central Asia they were then placed out of German reach. The Germans had planned to eliminate the Christian population of Poland entirely, starting with the intelligentsia and clergy, and continuing with the rest, through forced labour, mass sterilization, and killing. About three million Polish Christians became victims of this policy before the Germans were driven out. The area was eventually to be inhabited only by Germanic settlers. The Soviet Union, on the other hand, just wanted to turn all Poles, whether Christian or Jewish, into good Stalinist communists—however, they did not care how many hundreds of thousands were killed or deported in the process. They initiated this process during 1939–41, and resumed it after driving out the Germans in 1944–5.

There were both nationalist and communist resistance movements inside Poland when occupied, although the nationalist movement was crushed in the immediate postwar years. The fighting across the country in repeated waves left much of it in ruins, with the capital Warsaw systematically devastated by the Germans after a major uprising in the summer of 1944. Ironically, because of the rapid advance of the Red Army in the winter of 1944–5, some of the area in the north and west acquired by Poland was less devastated as the local German population was driven out and Poles, primarily from the eastern lands that had been turned over to the Soviet Union, settled there. In the new western territory several cities had also been devastated during the fighting, but the rural areas had not. After the war many Poles who had fled from the German or Soviet occupation refused to return because they did not want to live under the communist regime being installed there. The friction between Poles and Ukrainians continued during and after the war and included violence at the time and the forced resettlement of many Ukrainians after the war.

Denmark and Norway

If Poland was the country most changed by the war, Denmark was the least so. The government surrendered in 1940, but remained in administrative control of the country until August 1943; it survived, in part, the German assumption of more direct authority at that time, and saw the country liberated without fighting due to German surrender. There were, however, some arrests and a slowly increasing resistance. While the country's farm products helped feed Germany, the Danish people saved almost all Jews in Denmark by shipping them to Sweden or hiding them when the Germans decided to kill them in 1943. The Danish union with Iceland ended during the conflict. The latter and Greenland were effectively on the Allied side and neither saw significant hostilities.

The situation for Norway was fundamentally different from that of Denmark. There was fighting in 1940, which produced some destruction and, in the last months of the war, the retreating Germans in the northeastern portion of the country deliberately destroyed all buildings and facilities. Commando raids and local resistance caused damage at some localities; and with Norwegian shipping joining the Allies, many of their ships were sunk during the war. There was, however, little destruction of the main cities. Trondheim had been scheduled to become a major German city, grandiose plans that were ended by Allied victory. Internally there were controversies that left problems for after the war. The former minister, Vidkun Quisling, gave his name to the form of treason his support of the German invaders symbolized. He was executed after a postwar trial, and it represented one way of dealing with collaboration. Other victims of the war included many members of the resistance, who had been shot by the Germans, and a majority of the country's Jews, who had been killed when the second in command in the German foreign ministry, the state secretary Ernst von Weizsäcker, had waved off a Swedish offer to accept them. The bulk of Norwegian territory was, however, surrendered undamaged in 1945 by the substantial German force that had been stationed there at Hitler's orders to ward off an anticipated Allied invasion.

Holland, Belgium, Luxembourg, and France

Holland was the scene of fighting and bombing in 1940 and again in 1944–5. The Germans in some places had opened the dykes in 1944 to flood certain areas, and there was starvation in the winter of 1944–5. Resistance activity had led to extensive shooting of hostages, and most Jews had been carted off to killing centres. While the Dutch West Indies proved to be safe from both Japanese and Germans, the East Indies was occupied by the Japanese. There aspirations for independence had been stimulated by the disruption of prior colonial administration and liberation by American and Australian forces, and this meant that Dutch rule would end soon after its nominal restoration in 1945. The government in exile returned and had to face a society harshly affected by the conflict, especially during its last months.

Belgium had also been the site of serious fighting in 1940 and 1944–5, especially because of the German December 1944 Ardennes Offensive, known as the Battle of the Bulge, and this resulted in substantial destruction at some points. During the occupation, the Germans had shot many resisters, real or imagined, and had also slaughtered villagers in their final push. The fact that the king, unlike the queen of Holland, had remained behind created problems for the returning government-in-exile. Occupation had increased friction between the Walloon and Flemish elements in the population, and most of the country's Jews had been killed. It would take the country years to recover, and its internal frictions continued.

Luxembourg was quickly occupied in 1940 and annexed to Germany. There were various moves during the occupation to Germanize the area, and there was some fighting in the winter of

1944–5, but the physical damage was slight. The Grand Duchess, who had left, returned to the country as it regained independence.

The internal situation of France was extraordinarily complicated, and this affected both the immediate impact of war and the arguments, memories, and policies of the country afterwards. The fighting in May–June 1940 caused some damage, but nothing like that in the prior conflict. The Germans occupied the majority of the country, and in November 1942 occupied the rest. Large numbers of hostages had been shot, so had many real or imagined resisters, and numerous communities had been levelled to the ground. A portion of the Jewish population had been taken to killing centres, but the majority survived partly because of objections from French clergy and families who hid them and primarily because the Allied invasions of 1944 halted the deportation programme then under way. Those invasions and the bombing that preceded and accompanied them caused very substantial casualties among the civilian population and heavy damage, especially in the north and northeast of the country.

The Vichy regime installed in the unoccupied part of France tried to reverse all changes in the country since 1789 and left behind arguments, myths, and memories to agitate the country's public sphere for the next century. There was a rash of summary executions for real or imagined collaborators in 1944–5 and some trials of alleged collaborators afterwards. The resistance left behind its own myths for postwar debates. The vast French colonial empire, which had been divided between allegiance to Vichy and allegiance to the Free French leader de Gaulle, had been fought over in many cases, and was stirring with anti-colonial movements by the end of the war. Although France had a large agricultural part of the economy, there had been hunger in cities. The deported forced labourers for the most part returned home in 1945, while tens of thousands of German prisoners of war were retained in France as a new group of forced labourers to assist on farms and in reconstruction. The swift defeat of 1940 had been a major blow to the country's pride, and General de Gaulle did his best and his worst to revive it. His attempt to annex a piece of northwest Italy was thwarted by President Truman, but France did receive zones of occupation in Germany and Austria as well as sectors in Berlin and Vienna, had full control of the Saar area, held a seat on the Control Council for Germany, and was accorded a permanent seat on the Council of the United Nations organization.

Great Britain and its Commonwealth and Empire

Whatever divisions there had been in Britain before the war and during its first months disappeared in the spring and summer of 1940. The public rallied in the face of substantial civilian casualties from bombing, much destruction of cities, and rationing that lasted for a decade after victory. The series of calamitous defeats first at the hands of the Germans and subsequently the Japanese with the accompanying casualties shook the public but did not lead to a change of government between May 1940 and July 1945. As in France, military casualties were small compared with those of World War I. The government interned and subsequently released some Nazi sympathizers and a large number of refugees from Nazi Germany, having sent some of the latter to Canada and Australia. The death and destruction caused by the German V-1 and V-2 weapons in 1944–5 had tried the nerves of a population that had already suffered greatly, but since by then victory was in sight, the general effect was never what Hitler had hoped for. The people met what they called an 'American occupation' of hundreds of thousands of American servicemen with a mixture of joy and resentment, referring to them as 'over-paid, over-sexed, and over here'.

There would continue to be major restrictions on the life of the population, but the country's future was more substantially affected by two other effects of the war. The memory of the depressed situation of the country during the inter-war years and the hopes for a less class-divided and more economically egalitarian country led to a political landslide in the July 1945 election that brought the Labour Party to power. In international affairs, the exertions of Britain in World War II left it with nominal Great Power status but in reality it had been quite substantially weakened. The country's dominions not only asserted greater independence in diplomatic affairs but, especially in the case of Australia and New Zealand, had come to look instead to the United States for their security. The colonial empire was in turmoil, with the largest unit, India, clearly on the way to independence, and others in both Asia and Africa stirring in a similar direction. The two world wars had ended Britain's role as the world's super-power.

Italy

It had been difficult for Mussolini to explain to the Italian people why they should go to war again. Military defeat in east and north Africa as well as Greece followed by disastrous losses in early 1943 on the Eastern front dissolved practically all the public support the fascist system had ever held. The German decisions to assist Italy were resented rather than appreciated and had the critical result that from July 1943 to May 1945 the country was the scene of very destructive fighting. The loss of its colonial empire relieved the state of substantial expenses and thus contributed to the country's postwar economic recovery; but the main impacts of the war were a turn away from the monarchy that had united the country in the preceding century, the loss of some territory to Yugoslavia, and bitter memories of human and material losses along with residues from something approaching civil war in the conflict's last year.

The Soviet Union

The Soviet Union had been transformed by the war. Over 25 million of its people had been killed or had died from hunger and disease, while several million members of national minorities had been forced to move because of real or alleged inclinations to collaborate with the invader. Liberated prisoners of war and slave labourers were punished rather than welcomed home. Thousands of communities had been destroyed. On the other hand, the regime had acquired legitimacy in the eyes of the vast majority of the population for the first time, as the horrors of German occupation and prisoner of war policy had transformed Stalin from being a feared and hated dictator into the benign saviour of his people from a fate too terrible to contemplate. Although there was great damage to the economy in the western parts of the country, the evacuated and newly built factories in the Urals area and in central Asia continued to operate. What temporary relaxation the regime had allowed during the conflict in order to rally the population would be reversed rather than expanded, but this was off-set for many in the country by the state's new status in international affairs. There was pride in the role of the country in the great trial of war in spite of its enormous cost. Those in positions of authority at all levels could feel some satisfaction from the reversal of the results from Russia's fate in the prior war: it had gained, not lost territory, and it dominated Eastern and Southeastern Europe instead of losing all influence over its European neighbours. It had also regained some territory in east Asia that had been lost to Japan in 1905, but few in the country knew or cared about that.

Japan

The Japanese home front was severely strained by their eight years of war. The steady human toll that increased with bombing in 1944–5 became more difficult to bear as the increasingly effective Allied submarine campaign reduced supplies for the country's industry. The population became weary, but remained supportive of a regime that in 1942 had held elections in which some candidates not endorsed by the government had won seats in the Diet. The decision of the government to surrender spared the country millions of casualties, further bombing, destructive fighting in the home islands accompanied by the dropping of additional atomic bombs, and subsequent division into occupation zones and sectors. Those who had advised the emperor to order surrender may have been influenced by fear of a domestic political upheaval as deprivation and suffering became ever greater, but whatever the reason, the surrender implied a continuation of national unity under an American supreme commander. There was a British as well as an American occupation force, but the population quickly realized that these soldiers were more likely to assist than to bother them. The seizure by the Soviet Union of some small islands off the coast of Hokkaido and the deportation of their population remains a source of territorial dispute, but it affected only a tiny portion of a population relieved by the end of hostilities. Under a system modified primarily under American auspices, the country acquired a new constitution, independent trade unions, land reform, female suffrage, and a slowly rebounding economy.

China

China was both economically and politically transformed by the war's impact. The total human losses are not known but were most likely to number at least 15 million. There had been much destruction, but there had also been some new industrial development in the occupied and unoccupied portions of the country. The Soviets stripped much of the industry the Japanese had developed in Manchuria since seizing it in 1931, but the main impact of the years of fighting was that it aborted the effort of the Nationalist Party of Chiang Kai-shek to reconsolidate a state that had fallen into disarray early in the 20th century. As already mentioned, the main long-term effect of Japanese military operations, especially the 1944 Ichigo Offensive, was to enable the Chinese communists to win the civil war that soon followed the end of fighting between Japan and China. The unwillingness of postwar Japan to face up to its horrendous record of murder, rape, and devastation left in China, as well as elsewhere in east and southeast Asia, a heritage of hatred that has precluded the kind of reconciliation of peoples that a different policy and attitude on the part of postwar Germany has brought to Europe.

The United States

In the United States there was practically none of the division that had existed earlier and during World War I. The Japanese attack had ensured that local disputes, some rationing, efforts of the government at price control, and occasional strikes and lockouts never affected a general determination to see the war to a victorious conclusion. Bond drives, blood drives, and the collection of scrap metal and other items were readily accepted. The temporary incarceration of Japanese-Americans living in some American states, in order to conceal intelligence from the breaking of Japanese codes from any disloyal Japanese-Americans, created hardships for the victims and regrets in American society afterwards. The mid-term election of 1942 increased the strength of the Republican opposition, but President Roosevelt won a fourth term in the 1944 election so that a Democrat, Harry Truman, succeeded him on his death in April 1945. Three major long-term effects of wartime events must be noted. The deliberate effort of Roosevelt to accustom the public to a different role in the postwar world was successful; there would be no rejection of the peace settlement and international organization as there had been after World War I. Decisions made during the war to locate training camps and facilities as well as shipping construction in the southern, southwestern, and western portions of the country for reasons of climate and local geography produced a shifting of population distribution and the ensuing allocation of political power. Finally, there were significant changes set in motion in the status of women and of African-Americans.

Central and South America, neutrals, and technical developments

The countries of Central and South America had joined the Allies, with the exception of Argentina. Brazil and Mexico sent small contingents to fight, but otherwise their main role was to provide supplies and ships while denying these to the Axis powers. Some residents of German background were sent to the United States for internment, but there was relatively little domestic upheaval in these countries. At the end of the war, several of them received substantial numbers of German and Croatian war criminals escaping from possible trials, generally with the assistance of the Red Cross and members of the Vatican.

The European neutrals to a considerable degree had profited from the war by selling goods to both sides at high prices. Sweden had also allowed the transit of German soldiers, and Switzerland had been deeply involved in Nazi looting and financial operations. However, only Spain had sent a substantial number of soldiers to fight on Germany's side, but the survivors returned to a country still recovering from a bitter civil war.

In all major belligerents there had been significant developments in military technology and also medical practices applied during the war, which was of considerable postwar importance. New tanks, planes, warships, and artillery pieces had been built and utilized. Radar, jet airplanes, ballistic missiles, and nuclear weapons had been the most dramatic innovations employed during hostilities and developed further thereafter. The most extreme attempt at destruction, thousands of balloons carrying incendiaries, with which the Japanese had hoped to destroy the western parts of the United States and Canada, actually caused minimal casualties and destruction. Large-scale use of blood transfusions and the appearance of new drugs like penicillin had saved the lives of thousands of wounded and became standard elements of postwar medicine. So while the material destruction of the conflict had been immense, there were also some beneficial aspects to wartime developments.

Chapter 8
Allied victory, 1944–5

The Axis

By the spring of 1944, the German aim of world conquest was clearly no longer within reach. Hitler and those close to him hoped that either the alliance forged by those fighting against the Axis would fall apart or that a defeat of an Allied invasion in the West, which they expected to occur that year, would enable Germany to move large forces from the West to the Eastern front to crush a Red Army which had suffered very heavy casualties in prior fighting. At the same time, Germany planned to continue its high priority programme of slaughtering all Jews within its reach, whatever effect this might have on the conduct of military operations.

In Italy, the government that succeeded Mussolini and had surrendered to the Allies saw itself installed under Allied supervision in the south of the country. It recruited some troops to fight alongside the Allies, but could only watch as more of the country was devastated by the fighting and a puppet regime under Mussolini was established by the Germans in northern Italy where partisans fought the Germans and each other. The Japanese government had once received Germany's agreement to divide Asia at the 70th degree longitude, but even the success of the Ichigo offensive in the summer of 1944 could not offset defeats in India, the Marianas, and the southwest Pacific, or the increasing shipping losses on the sea lanes from southeast Asia. Fighting on as fiercely as possible appeared to be the only option.

The Allies

The Western Allies intended to fight until the Axis powers surrendered unconditionally. This time there would be no pretence that the defeated had not actually been defeated as the Germans had argued had been the case after World War I. The American government leaders were also determined that their country would not abandon the world as they had done after World War I but that instead its people would become engaged in an international organization. The Soviet regime's full ambitions cannot be described accurately until the presidential archive in Moscow is opened (hopefully before the paper it is recorded on has deteriorated beyond recall), but some points are clear. The regime was planning to extend its rule and beyond that its influence as far into Europe as possible. It was to join an international organization in the hope of thereby precluding a renewed invasion by a resurgent Germany although it had earlier been ejected from the League of Nations. One must recall that all leaders of the time were strongly influenced by the fact that a defeated Germany had nonetheless made a second bid for world domination after a mere 20 years, and they therefore focused attention and plans on preventing a further repetition of that experience.

The Allies had essentially agreed at their conference in Teheran in Iran that they would carry out 1944 offensives on all major fronts in Europe, specifically including an invasion across the Channel to be supported by an invasion on the Mediterranean coast of France. In spite of continued doubts by Churchill, the plans for 'Overlord', the cross-Channel invasion, went forward; and in the face of even stronger British objections, so did plans for the French Riviera landing, code-named first 'Anvil' and later 'Dragoon'. The correct assumption of the Allies was that essentially simultaneous major offensives in Italy, France, and on the Eastern front would prevent Germany from shifting forces from any portion of Europe to ward off offensives elsewhere. Furthermore, successful deception operations in the West kept German troops waiting in the Calais area and in Norway for landings that never occurred, while Soviet deception kept German reserves awaiting a Soviet offensive against German Army Group North Ukraine when the big blow was to hit Army Group Centre.

Chronologically, first the Allies launched a major offensive in Italy on 11 May. American and British troops ground their way through the German defences and joined with those who had landed in January at Anzio. Contrary to plans and good sense, American commander General Mark Clark raced for Rome instead of cutting off a large part of the German force. Rome was liberated on 4 June, but the Allies had to slog their way north to clear north-central Italy. The offensive in Italy nevertheless prevented the Germans from moving troops to other fronts threatened soon after and enabled the Allies to employ some units hitherto based in Italy for the landing in southern France.

On 6 June, British, American, and Canadian forces landed on five beaches of Normandy, an operation made possible by their prior victory in the air and on the oceans. Determined German resistance slowed their uniting the bridgeheads and breaking into the interior of France, but in the last week of July the Americans broke through at the western end of the Normandy front and pushed rapidly into the French interior as well as into Brittany (Map 12). An attempt on 20 July by German opponents of Hitler to kill the dictator failed, and, with only one exception, all German higher commanders rallied to the leader who had bribed them, rather than to General Ludwig Beck, leader of the military opposition and former chief of the general staff. In mid-August American and French armies landed on the French Mediterranean coast and pushed north after seizing the key ports of Toulon and Marseille that then became critical for the Allied supply situation. Paris was liberated by the drive from Normandy, and soon after the

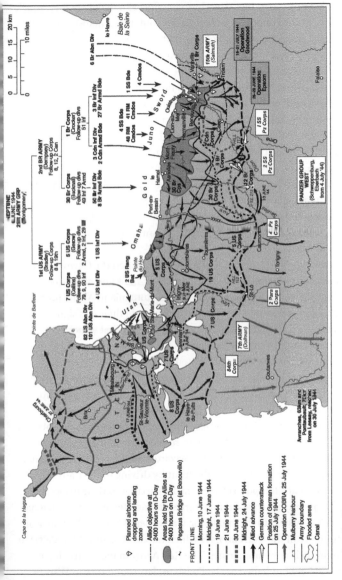

12. Overlord

two landing forces met. The German effort at a major counter-attack to cut off the American force breaking out of Normandy had failed, and the wrecking and/or holding on to the ports to keep the Allies from supplying and reinforcing their armies contributed to slowing Allied offensives in the autumn but still could not defeat them. The September attempt of the Allies to jump the Rhine River barrier at the northern end of the front by combining a series of three airborne assaults to seize bridges over the river's branches and drive across them into the Netherlands and northern Germany failed when the Germans crushed the northernmost airborne division. The Allies nevertheless continued advancing in some sectors, and the first important German city, Aachen, was taken by the Americans on 21 October. German reinforcements and pre-war fortifications near the German border slowed the Allies while the Germans secretly prepared a major counter-offensive.

On the Eastern front, the Red Army had cleared the Germans out of most of the Ukraine in the first months of 1944 and also retook the Crimea in April. A major offensive into Romania in April and May was, however, turned back by the Germans in their last significant tactical victory in the East. In June the Soviets first struck at Finland and in a series of offensives forced Finland to sue for an armistice that was signed in September. Because of a German operation, the Finns ended up fighting their former allies. The main carefully prepared Soviet offensive struck German Army Group Centre on 22 June. Operation 'Bagration' produced Germany's greatest defeat of the war as the whole Army Group was demolished with tens of thousands of German soldiers becoming prisoners (Map 13). The Red Army drove forward rapidly and cut off German units at the northern end of the front by driving to the Baltic Sea. The Germans temporarily reopened a corridor to their troops, but subsequently a major German force was isolated in western Latvia which they held to the end of the war, ordered to do so by Hitler on the advice of the German navy which needed to control the Baltic to run in their new submarines. The Red Army in the centre drove into Poland but halted as the Polish underground rose in Warsaw.

Key

Front line by Dec 1943
Front line by mid-June 1944
Front line by end Dec 1944
xxxxx– Army Group/Front boundary
Surrounded German armies
International boundary 21 June 1941
6th German formations
1st Balt. Soviet formations

0   100   200   300   400   500 km
0   100   200   300   250 miles

[1]terminated Feb 1944
[2]activated 21 April 1944, terminated 16 Oct 1944
[3]terminated Feb 1945
[4]WEST FRONT before April 1945
[5]BELORUSSIAN FRONT before Feb 1944
[6]deactivated 1944, reactivated Aug 1944
[7]became ARMY GROUP SOUTH UKRAINE, April 1944, which became ARMY GROUP SOUTH Sept 1944
[8]became ARMY GROUP NORTH UKRAINE, April 1944, which became ARMY GROUP A, Sept 1944
[9]renamed ARMY GROUP COURLAND, Jan 1945
[10]renamed ARMY GROUP NORTH, Jan 1945. Disbanded 2 April 1945
[11]renamed ARMY GROUP CENTRE, Jan 1945

13. German–Soviet War 1943–44

The bridgeheads across the Vistula and Narew rivers secured by the Red Army would be utilized for their subsequent winter offensive. In the meantime, a successful drive into Romania was met by Romania switching sides in late August, thereby facilitating Soviet occupation of Bulgaria and launching an offensive into Hungary. As the latter had attempted to find a way out of the war, it had been occupied by German troops in March 1944. This gave the Germans a temporary opportunity to kill a substantial part of Hungary's large Jewish community, but then obliged them to try to defend the country against the Red Army.

Winter 1944–45 in Europe

In mid-December the Germans launched their last reserves against the Americans in the Ardennes, hoping to retake the important port of Antwerp, drive the United States out of the European war as its home front collapsed under the impact of a major defeat, achieve a similar effect on the British, and thereby free massive forces for the Eastern front. The offensive surprised and temporarily pushed back the Americans in what became known as the Battle of the Bulge, but turned into a major defeat as the Americans held and the Germans lost heavily in soldiers and equipment. In February the Western Allies resumed major offensives, and since the Germans had committed and lost much of their forces on the left bank of the Rhine river, the Allies soon crossed that last potential barrier and drove into Germany.

The Soviets had resumed their offensives at the central part of the frontline and in Hungary in January. They drove into Germany and Austria, and in spite of German counter-attacks in both places they surrounded Berlin in April while meeting the Americans at Torgau south of that city. The German forces in Italy surrendered in early May. Admiral Dönitz, who succeeded Hitler on 30 April upon the latter's suicide, ordered a general unconditional surrender on 8 May. With minimal exceptions, all German land, sea, and air units followed the surrender directive.

Allied offensives in east Asia and the Pacific

In the war in east Asia and the Pacific, the British completed the reconquest of Burma and prepared for a landing on the coast of Malaya (Operation Zipper) scheduled for September 1945. The American successful landings in the Marianas, the northwest coast of New Guinea, the island Morotai, and the Palau islands prepared the way for the landing on Leyte in the central Philippines in October 1944 (Map 14). Bitter and lengthy fighting on that island followed, as did a major naval battle as the Japanese tried desperately to defeat the landing and the American naval force supporting it. Though slowed by the reinforced Japanese, the Americans took Leyte only to discover that it was not appropriate for the air bases that were needed to support the planned invasion of Luzon, and a landing on Mindoro in mid-December had to follow. The naval battle came to be a major American victory in which the extraordinary bravery of American escort carriers and destroyers combined with a misreading of the situation by Japanese naval commander Kurita Takeo—who thought that he was facing the main American fleet—offset the decision of American Admiral William Halsey to chase after a Japanese decoy fleet instead of protecting the landing force. By a supreme irony, in the portion of the naval battle fought in Surigao Strait, most of the American battleships used had been among those that the Japanese had imagined they had 'sunk' in Pearl Harbor on 7 December 1941, but which had in fact been raised, repaired, and returned to service.

The American invasion of the northern island of Luzon began in January 1945, and it led to the bitterly fought liberation of Manila, where the Japanese forces murdered and raped thousands in March 1945, as they had done in Singapore in February 1942—under the same commander, Yamashita Tomoyuki. The latter, with a substantial force, continued to hold a portion of northern Luzon up until the Japanese surrender, while the Americans undertook a series of landings on other islands in the central and southern Philippines.

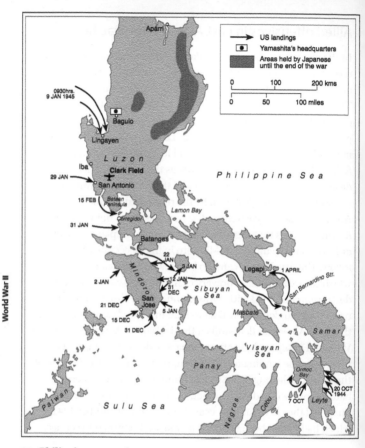

14. Philippines campaign 1944–45

It was during the campaign in the Philippines that the Japanese initiated the employment of suicide airplanes called *kamikaze*. These tried to dive into American ships and caused serious damage to many of them. The subsequent employment of small suicide planes held from above by larger planes that carried them to their release point proved much less effective. The Japanese also developed and increasingly utilized suicide submarines (*kaiten*) and other forms of suicide ships, but again with little effect. The employment of thousands of incendiary balloons, mentioned earlier, sent across the Pacific Ocean to set fire to the forests and cities of western Canada and the United States was the most destructive concept of any country in the war but had the least impact in practice.

In February 1945, American Marines landed on Iwo Jima in the Bonin Islands between the Philippines and the Japanese home islands where the Japanese had several airfields. A bitter and costly campaign brought the island under American control. To secure a major base for the planned invasions of the Japanese home islands, the Americans formed a new army and landed on Okinawa, the largest island in the Ryukyu chain, on 1 April 1945 (Map 15). By that time, the British were able to play a substantial role in the Pacific War and contributed a portion of the covering fleet for what became the bloodiest battle for both the American army and navy in the war against Japan. The fighting, primarily on the southern portion of the island, lasted for over three months, but the island was eventually completely taken, its important airfields actually having been seized in the first days.

During the fighting on Okinawa, Australian and American forces initiated operations against the Japanese on islands they had conquered in the Dutch East Indies. In a series of landings on Borneo in May to July 1945, much of that island with its important oil wells was taken, and a landing on Java was planned for September. Substantial Japanese forces remained in much of the Indies until their surrender in September.

The final defeat of Japan

The plans for ending the war against Japan, 'Operation Downfall', included landings on the southern island of Kyushu in November 1945, 'Operation Olympic', to provide bases for landings in and near Tokyo Bay, 'Operation Coronet', in March 1946. In both

15. The Okinawa campaign 1945

operations, the initial force would be American, and in 'Coronet'
British Commonwealth and French divisions would be included in
the follow-up. The expectation of an attack from China and
Formosa/Taiwan had been obviated by the Japanese 'Ichigo'
offensive, but major assistance was expected from Soviet armies
attacking and thus tying down Japanese forces in Manchuria,
Korea, and China as well as attacking and bombing the home

islands from the north. A major concern was that after occupation of the home islands, the Japanese troops, numbering over a million, in east and southeast Asia and on islands and portions of islands in the Pacific would continue to fight until death, which the Allies would have to inflict in 'Post-Coronet Operations'. Unlike the fighting in Europe and north Africa, the fighting against Japan had led to only tiny numbers of individual Japanese soldiers surrendering—mostly when wounded or when they were in fact forcibly recruited local inhabitants—and no whole units ever did surrender as had been seen in Stalingrad and Tunisia.

The Allies called upon the Japanese government to surrender in July 1945, from Potsdam—a deliberate choice of timing and location. When this demand and similar advice from Japanese diplomats of which the Americans knew from decoded intercepts were 'unanimously rejected' by the governing council in Tokyo, the American president Harry Truman in accord with secretary of war Henry Stimson and with the prior agreement of both British and Soviet governments decided to utilize newly available atomic bombs to try to shock the Japanese into surrendering. In what was originally seen as a race with Germany, the Western powers had continued work to develop atomic bombs when they concluded that the Germans were not getting anywhere in this field. The Americans, who planned to use the available atomic bombs in support of 'Olympic', decided to use one, and, if necessary, a second one, on Japanese cities, and if that did not produce a surrender, they would save those becoming available thereafter for 'Olympic'.

The Japanese government not only rejected the Potsdam call to surrender but agreed on a plan to defend against invasions—whose locations they correctly anticipated—assuming that Japanese willingness to accept 20 million casualties would discourage the Allies from their surrender demand. Tokyo tried unsuccessfully to obtain Soviet support for a negotiated end to the war or to have that country switch sides. The leaders in Tokyo were also not moved by massive American air raids, primarily from the

Marianas, which destroyed large parts of major Japanese cities and caused, especially in Tokyo itself, massive casualties. The second atomic bomb led to a split in the governing council. Half, impressed by the fact that one plane dropping one bomb could now accomplish what previously had taken hundreds of planes dropping thousands of bombs, concluded that the Allies could now kill all or almost all in the home islands and did not need to invade. They therefore abandoned the defence plan in favour of surrender. Under these circumstances, Emperor Hirohito, perhaps influenced by advisors concerned about a possible domestic upheaval and the Soviet entrance into the Pacific War, met with the council and personally ordered a surrender.

An attempted coup by those wanting to continue fighting failed when war minister Anami Korechika, torn between his policy preference for fighting on and loyalty to the Emperor, committed suicide rather than join the coup. The Allies made it easier for the Japanese to surrender unconditionally by stating that they could keep the imperial institution if they wanted to do so, although it would now be under Allied control, and by, at British suggestion, allowing designated officials instead of the Emperor to sign the surrender. Hirohito, in turn, sent emissaries, including family members, to Japanese commanders in the field to insist on surrender everywhere. There were no 'Post-Coronet' operations, and Japan was not divided into zones of occupation with Tokyo divided into sectors. American and British Commonwealth troops occupied the country, but the country's government and administration remained in Japanese hands, guided and reformed by directives from the Supreme Commander of the Allied Powers (SCAP), General MacArthur. Tiny numbers of Japanese soldiers held out into the 1970s, but generally the Emperor's surrender order was obeyed.

Conclusion

When the greatest war in history ended, around 60 million people had been killed, the majority of them civilians. The largest number, over 25 million, was in the Soviet Union, with a figure of at least 15 million in China. There were huge losses in other countries, but none had been ravaged, shoved about, looted, and decimated more than Poland. Massive destruction and economic dislocation characterized much of Europe, east Asia, southeast Asia, and portions of north Africa. The arrival of such new weapons as Germany's ballistic missile, the V-2, and the American atomic bomb suggested that any future war between major powers might well bring about the end of humanity on the planet.

The war and its ending also brought about enormous population movements. Millions of prisoners of war and enslaved labourers struggled to return to their homes and over some years generally managed to do so. On the other hand, some from Eastern Europe did not want to return to countries that had fallen under Soviet domination, and Jewish survivors from Poland discovered that their return was not wanted and dangerous, so they preferred to move to Palestine, which the British attempted to keep closed. Additional millions of Europeans were displaced by the new boundaries established by the victors. Since the Germans had endlessly condemned the effort to adjust boundaries to people at Versailles in 1919 and insisted on the principle of adjusting people to boundaries instead, that procedure was applied to Germany. Some 12 million Germans lost their homes in former eastern Germany and Czechoslovakia, Poland, and other countries of East and Southeast Europe in the largest population movement ever in a short time. Italy lost its colonial empire and some land to Yugoslavia. Several million Japanese from that country's empire were moved back to the home islands. After surrender, Japan remained a unit; it was not divided into occupation zones nor was its capital divided into sectors, as occurred with Germany and Austria and their capitals. Only some tiny islands off the northeast coast of Hokkaido were annexed by the Soviet Union and their inhabitants deported, an issue that has prevented the signing of peace between the two countries into the 21st century.

The Allies were faced with the issue of how to deal with war criminals, who they had promised to try and punish. At this time many who had reason to fear justice did what they could to hide, assume new identities, or escape to South America with Vatican assistance. The newly liberated countries faced not only a massive reconstruction problem but also the question of how to deal with those who had collaborated with the occupying forces. Most of the defeated countries found themselves with reparations to pay, and ironically a truncated and much damaged Germany paid much more than a larger and essentially untouched Germany had done after World War I. In addition to creating new and improved weapons of destruction, the war effort had also brought new developments in medicine as well as a means of air transportation, the jet engine, which was to transform postwar travel.

If victory had been enormously costly, the alternative the world would have faced was so horrendous as to make the cost necessary, in retrospect: the genocidal policy applied by the Germans to Jews and Roma prefigured even vaster systematic killing, starvation, and forced sterilization of enormous masses, with the eventual plan that only the so-called Aryans should inhabited an Earth on which they worshipped only themselves. The conflict had, on the other hand, simultaneously speeded up the process of decolonization, a process that came to include neutral Spain and Portugal as well as the participating colonial powers. The conflict did provide the Soviet Union with a new sense of legitimacy in the eyes of the vast majority of its inhabitants, but that would fade with time. A different world emerged from its greatest conflict, one that by its nature, and especially by its conclusion, warned all to be most cautious thereafter.

Further reading

On the war as a whole, there is Gerhard L. Weinberg, *A World at Arms: A Global History of World War II*, 2nd edn, New York, 2005. For the war's origins, there are the same author's *Hitler's Foreign Policy 1933–1939: The Road to World War II*, New York, 2005; and Zara Steiner, *The Triumph of the Dark: European International History 1933–1939*, Oxford, 2011. While the literature on the war is enormous, a very helpful guide to its key figures will be found in Mark M. Boatner III, *The Biographical Dictionary of World War II*, Novato, CA, 1996.

Readings on each campaign cannot be listed here, but for the first, see Alexander B. Rossino, *Hitler Strikes Poland: Blitzkrieg, Ideology, and Atrocity*, Lawrence, 2003. The crushing of France is reviewed in Ernest R. May, *Strange Victory: Hitler's Conquest of France*, New York, 2000. Michael Korda, *With Wings Like Eagles: A History of the Battle of Britain*, New York, 2009, offers a recent survey. For the German invasion of the Soviet Union and the subsequent fighting on the Eastern front there are numerous excellent works by Robert Citino, David Glantz, David Stahel, and Earl Ziemke. On the fighting in Italy, the British and American official histories offer excellent surveys and Richard Lamb's *War in Italy 1943–1945: A Brutal Story*, New York, 1994, provides a necessary supplement. It should be noted that the British official history, entitled *The Mediterranean and Middle East* (vols I–V), provides helpful coverage of all aspects including north Africa, Iraq, and Syria, as well as operations in Italy.

The fighting in the West in 1944–5 is introduced by Alan F. Wilt, *The Atlantic Wall 1941–1944*, New York, 2004, which can be followed by Carlo D'Este, *Decision in Normandy*, New York, 1994, and Theodore A. Wilson (ed.), *D-Day 1944*, Lawrence, 1994. The subsequent fighting can be followed in Ian Kershaw, *The End: The Defiance and Destruction of Hitler's Germany, 1944–45*, New York, 2011, and Stephen G. Fritz, *Endkampf: Soldiers, Civilians, and the Death of the Third Reich*, Lexington, 2004.

For the two sides of the war in the air, good introductions are Tami Davis Biddle, *Rhetoric and Reality in Air Warfare: The Evolution of British and American Ideas about Strategic Bombing, 1914–1945*, Princeton, 2002, and Edward D. Westermann, *Flak: German Anti-Aircraft Defenses, 1914–1945*, Lawrence, 2001. Nathan Miller, *War at Sea: A Naval History of World War II*, New York, 1995, is well supplemented by Howard D. Grier, *Hitler/Dönitz and the Baltic Sea: The Third Reich's Last Hope, 1944–1945*, Annapolis, 2007. A careful analysis of Germany's armed forces will be found in Wolfram Wette, *The Wehrmacht: History, Myth, Reality*, trans. by Deborah Lucas Schneider, Cambridge, MA, 2006; on the country's military leaders one can find much insight in Geoffrey Megargee, *Inside Hitler's High Command*, Lawrence, 2000; while Donald M. McKale, *Hitler's Shadow War: The Holocaust and World War II*, New York, 2002, offers an excellent introduction to the title's subject. The effect of the Holocaust on German military operations is the subject of a book by Yaron Pasher forthcoming from the University Press of Kansas (Lawrence, 2014). Germany's occupation of much of Europe is covered by Mark Mazower, *Hitler's Empire: How the Nazis Ruled Europe*, New York, 2008. The complicated issues of Italy's internal divisions after the 1943 surrender are delineated in Claudio Pavone, *A Civil War: A History of the Italian Resistance*, trans. by Peter Levy and David Broder, ed. and with an introduction by Stanislao G. Pugliese (London, 2013).

Two fine surveys of the war in the Pacific are John Costello, *The Pacific War*, New York, 1982; and Ronald H. Spector, *Eagle against the Sun: The American War with Japan*, 1985. A good place to start on the beginning of Japan's expansion of its war with China is Alan D. Zimm, *Attack on Pearl Harbor: Strategy, Combat, Myths, Deceptions*, Havertown, PA, 2011. The key turning point is covered in

Jonathan Parshall and Antony Tully, *Shattered Sword: The Untold Story of the Battle of Midway*, Washington, DC, 2005. The first American offensive—and the longest battle in American history—is reported very well in Richard B. Frank, *Guadalcanal: The Definitive Account of the Landmark Battle*, New York, 1990. An excellent introduction to the campaign in the southwest Pacific is D. Clayton James, *The Years of MacArthur*, Vol. II, *1941-1945*, Boston, 1975. On the fighting in southeast Asia, there is the helpful survey of Louis Allen, *Burma: The Longest War 1941-1945*, London, 1984. For a culminating event in the American drive across the Pacific, see H. P. Willmott, *The Battle of Leyte Gulf: The Last Fleet Action*, Bloomington, 2005. The air attacks on Japan are well summarized in Barrett Tillman, *Whirlwind: The Air War against Japan 1942-1945*, New York, 2010. On the final stages of the war in the Pacific, excellent surveys are Richard B. Frank, *Downfall: The End of the Imperial Japanese Empire*, New York, 1999, and D. M. Giangreco, *Hell to Pay: Operation DOWNFALL and the Invasion of Japan, 1945-1947*, Annapolis, 2009.

Good introductions to the Japanese armed forces will be found in Edward J. Drea, *Japan's Imperial Army: Its Rise and Fall, 1853-1945*, Lawrence, 2009; Paul S. Dull, *A Battle History of the Imperial Japanese Navy (1941-1945)*, Annapolis, 1978; and M. G. Sheftall, *Blossoms in the Wind: Human Legacies of the Kamikaze*, New York, 2005. For a survey of Japan's occupation policies in east Asia and their repercussions, one still needs to turn to *The Far East 1942-1946* by F. C. Jones, Hugh Borton, and B. R. Pearn in the 'Survey of International Affairs', Oxford, 1955.

The war aims of leaders of the belligerents are summarized in Gerhard L. Weinberg, *Visions of Victory: The Hopes of Eight World War II Leaders*, New York, 2005. For the relationship of five key leaders with their military commanders there are helpful introductory accounts in Helmut Heiber and David M. Glantz, eds., *Hitler and His Generals: Military Conferences 1942-1945*, New York, 2002; John Gooch, *Mussolini and His Generals: The Armed Forces and Italian Foreign Policy, 1922-1940*, Cambridge, 2007; Raymond Callahan, *Churchill and His Generals*, Lawrence, 2007; Stephen Roskill, *Churchill and the Admirals*, Barnsley, 1977; Seweryn Bialer, ed., *Stalin and His Generals: Soviet Military Memoirs of*

World War II, London, 1970; Harold Shukman, ed., *Stalin's Generals*, London, 1993; and Eric Larrabee, *Commander in Chief: Franklin Delano Roosevelt, His Lieutenants, and Their War*, New York, 1987.

For further suggestions on many aspects of the war, readers will want to consult the 'Bibliographic Essay', pp. 921–44 in the first book listed above.

Index

A

Aachen 114
Abyssinia (Ethiopia) 1, 45
Admiralty Islands 73, 96
Alaska 76, 77
Albania 46
Aleutian Islands 94
Algeria 87
Anami Korechika 122
Antonescu, Ion 53
Antwerp 116
Anvil (Operation) 111
Anzio 112
Archangel 59
Ardennes Offensive, see Battle of
   the Bulge
Assam 95
Atomic weapons 106-7, 121-2
Attu 77, 94
Australia 2, 14, 16, 51, 67, 71-3, 77,
   96, 102, 104, 119
Austria 13, 104, 116
Azores 97

B

Badoglio, Pietro 93
Bagration (Operation) 114
Baltic Sea 89, 114

Barbarossa (Operation) 52-65
Bataan 72
Battle of Britain 43-4, 67
Battle of the Atlantic 24, 31, 87,
   89, 97
Battle of the Bulge 102, 116
Battle of the Coral Sea 76-8
Battle of the Java Sea 73
Beck, Ludwig 112
Beda Fromm 46
Belgium 33-5, 102
Berlin 58, 104, 116
Bessarabia 39
Bismarck Islands 73
Bizerte 87
"Blitz" 41, 43
Bonin Islands 119
Borneo 73, 119
British Somaliland 45
Bucovina 39
Bulgaria 47, 79, 116
Burma 70, 73, 95-6, 117
Burma Road 66, 67

C

Cairo Conference 97
Calais 112
Canada 2, 14, 19, 24, 40, 76, 89,
   109, 112, 119

Cape Matapan 46
Caroline Islands 73
Caribbean 76
Casablanca Conference 88–9
Caucasus 51, 81, 82, 84
Central America 76
Ceylon (Sri Lanka) 76
Chamberlain, Neville 15, 31, 44
Chetniks 96
Chiang Kai-shek 66, 107
Chile 76
China 1, 12, 66–7, 94–5, 107, 120, 123
Cholm 63
Churchill, Winston 15, 31, 40, 42, 46, 88, 111
Citadel (Operation) 86–9
Clark, Mark 112
Columbia 76
Coronet (Operation) 119
Corregidor 72
Crete 50
Crimea 114
Croatia 58
Czechoslovakia 14–15, 124

D

Dakar 67
Danzig 16, 23
Darlan, François 87, 88
DeGaulle, Charles 40, 51, 88, 103, 104
Demyansk 63
Denmark 28–30, 96, 101
Dill, Sir John 40
Dönitz, Karl 79, 87, 116
Doolittle, James 77
Dowding, Sir Hugh 44
Downfall (Operation) 119
Dragoon (Operation) 111
Dunkirk 38, 40
Dutch East Indies 68, 70, 73, 96, 102, 119
Dutch Harbor 77
Dutch West Indies 102

E

Ecuador 76
Egypt 45, 47, 87
Eisenhower, Dwight 87
El Alamein 87
Estonia 27, 39, 57, 59–60
"euthanasia" 97–8

F

Finland 27, 39, 45, 52–4, 65, 114
Foggia 93
Formosa (Taiwan) 120
France 12–14, 18, 19, 34–51, 93, 102–4, 111–14
  colonial empire 2, 67
Franco, Francisco 38, 58
Free French 51, 67, 88, 103
French Indo-China 66–9

G

Gamelin, Maurice 34
Gehlen, Reinhard 86
Gela 91
Germany 10, 12, 42–3, 52, 89–90, 95, 98–9, 104, 107, 110–12, 114, 116, 123–4
  atomic weapons 121
  and Japan 37, 69, 76, 78–9, 97
  opposition to Nazi regime 32, 33, 45, 112
  Reichstag (parliament) 61–2, 78
  and Soviet Union, 48–55, 61–73, 111, 115
  and United States 66, 78
Gilbert Islands 73, 96
Giraud, Henri 88
Göring, Hermann 35, 98
Great Britain 12–17, 23, 31–2, 41–2, 47, 48, 56, 93, 96, 104–5, 112, 119
  1945 election 105
  colonial empire 105

and Finland 65
and Japan 56-61
and Soviet Union 58-9
Greece 47-50, 93
Greenland 31
Grozhny 82
Guadalcanal 78, 84
Guam 70, 72

H

Haile Selassie 45
Haiphong-Hanoi railway 66-7
Haj Amin al-Husayni 51, 54
Halder, Franz 43, 54
Halifax, Lord 31, 41
Halsey, William 117
Hamburg 89
Hawaii 77, 78
Himalayas 95
Hindenburg, Paul von 10
Hirohito, Emperor 122
Hitler, Adolf 10-20, 25-6, 32-41,
    43-4, 47, 52-4, 55, 57, 58,
    60-3, 67, 69, 70, 76, 79, 83, 87,
    89, 98, 102, 110, 114, 116
Hoepner, Erich, 61-2
Holland 33-5, 67, 102
Holocaust 22, 53-4, 59, 98-103,
    110, 116, 123, 124
Homma Masaharu 72
Hong Kong 72
Hopkins, Harry 59
Hull, Cordell 69
'Hump, The' 95
Hungary 16, 45, 50, 58, 79,
    81, 116
Husky (Operation) 86, 88,
    91-2, 93

I

Iceland 31
Ichigo (Operation) 95, 107, 110
Imphal-Kohima 95

India 2, 19, 51, 71, 74, 95,
    105, 110
Indian Ocean 73
Iran 59
Iraq 50-1
Irish Republic 19
Italian Somaliland 45
Italy 2, 38, 45-7, 58, 69, 81, 84, 88,
    91, 93, 97, 105, 110-12, 124
    and Abyssinia 1-2, 45
    and United States 79
Iwo Jima 119

J

Japan 12, 22, 106, 107, 110,
    118-19, 124
    and China 1, 66-7
    and Germany 67, 69, 76,
        78-9, 97
    occupation of 106, 121
    and Soviet Union 61, 68, 107,
        121, 124
    surrender 121-2
    war with Great Britain, Holland,
        the United States 56-61,
        94-6, 108
Java 73, 119
Jews, see Holocaust

K

Kaiten 119
Kamikaze 118-19
Kasserine Pass 88
Kenya 45
Kharkov 84
Kiev 58
Kiska 77
Kokoda Trail 77, 94
Korea 120
Kuban bridgehead 84
Kurita Takeo 117
Kursk 86
Kyushu 119

L

Latvia 27, 39, 57, 59–60, 114
Laval, Pierre 39
League of Nations 111
Lend–Lease 42, 86
Leningrad 53, 57, 86
Leyte 117
Libya 46–7, 50, 87, 88
Lithuania 16, 27, 38–9, 57, 59–60
Lloyd George, David 41
Luxembourg 33–5, 102
Luzon 117

M

MacArthur, Douglas 72, 94, 122
Madagascar 73–4
Maginot Line 34
Malaya 59, 68, 70–1, 117
Malta 50
Manchuria 1, 61, 107, 120
Manila 72, 117
Mariana Islands 73, 96, 110, 117, 122
Marketgarden (Operation) 114
Marseille 112
Matsuoka Yosuke 67
medicine 109
Midway 77–8, 94
Milne Bay 77
Mindoro 117
Molotov, Vyacheslav 45
Montgomery, Bernard 91
Morocco 87
Morotai 117
Moscow 53, 57–8, 60, 61, 81, 82
Moscow Conference 97
Murmansk 25, 31, 57, 59
Mussolini, Benito 12, 15, 19, 38, 39, 45–7, 58, 91, 105, 110

N

Naples 93
Narew river 116
Narvik 28–30
New Britain Islands, 73
New Guinea 73, 77, 94, 96, 117
New Zealand 2, 19, 67, 76, 105
Nimitz, Chester 94
Nomonhan (Khalkin-Gol) 22
Normandy 112–14
Norway 26–32, 41, 53, 96, 101, 112
Novorossisk 82

O

Okinawa 119–20
Olympic (Operation) 119, 121
Operation Blue 81–6
Operation Uranus 83–6
Orel 86
Oster, Hans 33
Overlord (Operation) 87, 110, 112–14

P

Palau Islands 117
Palermo 91
Palestine 123
Paris 112
Patton, George 91
Paulus, Friedrich 84
Pearl Harbor 70, 117
Peru 76
Pétain, Philippe 39, 41
Philippines 67, 68, 70, 72–3, 94, 96, 117–18
Poland 3, 7–8, 16–24, 99–100, 114–15, 123, 124
Port Moresby 76, 77
Portugal 96, 125
Post-Coronet (Operations) 121, 122

Q

Quisling, Vidkun 28, 30, 101

R

Rabaul 73
Raeder, Erich 25–6
Rangoon 73
Rashid Ali al-Gaylani 51
resistance movements in occupied areas 96
Rhine river 114, 116
Ribbentrop, Joachim von 18
Roma 124
Romania 39, 45–7, 53, 58, 65, 79, 81–3, 114–15
Rome 112
Rommel, Erwin 47, 50
Roosevelt, Franklin 18, 31, 41–2, 45, 59, 69–70, 72, 79, 88, 108
Rosenberg, Alfred 64, 98
Rostov 61, 82
Rotterdam 35
Rundstedt, Gerd von 35
Ryukyu Islands 119

S

Saar territory 104
Saipan 96
Salerno 93
Siberia 76
Sicily, see Husky
Singapore 67, 69, 71–2
Slovakia 58
Smolensk 57
Solomon Islands 94, 96
Soviet Union 13, 17–18, 22, 25, 27, 28, 39, 44–5, 93, 94, 99–100, 105–6, 111, 123, 125
and China 66, 68, 107
German invasion 50–5, 112, 114–15
and Japan 67, 68, 106, 119–21, 124
partisan warfare 64, 86
Spain 58, 97, 125
Civil War 1, 2, 38
Stalin, Josef 13, 17, 18, 25, 39, 45, 54, 58, 60, 63, 82, 84
Stalingrad 63, 82–4, 87, 89
Stimson, Henry 121
Strait of Messina 91
strategic bombing campaign 88–90
Surigao Strait 117
Sweden 25, 26, 31, 53, 97, 101
Switzerland 97
Syria 51

T

Taiwan/Formosa 120
Takoradi 46
tanks 52–3, 55, 84, 86
Taranto 46
Tarawa 96
Teheran Conference 96, 111
Thailand 70
Tikhvin 61
Tito 96
Tobruk 50
Tojo Hideki 76
Tokyo 77, 121
Torch (Operation) 87–9
Torgau 116
Toulon 112
Transnistria 65
Trondheim 26, 30
Truman, Harry 104, 108, 121
Tunis 87
Tunisia 87–9
Turkey 97

U

Ukraine 53, 57–60, 65, 86, 114
unconditional surrender doctrine 88, 111

Union of South Africa 2, 14, 19
United Nations 80, 104
United States 12, 25–6, 41–2,
    79–80, 94–7, 108
  1944 election 108
  and Finland 65
  and Japan Chap. 5, 109,
    117–19
  and Soviet Union 59, 63
Uranus, *see* Operation Uranus

V

V–1 and V–2 104
Vatican 124
Venezuela 76
Vichy 51, 87, 103
Victor Emmanuel III, 91
Vienna 104
Vistula river 116

W

Wake 70, 72
war criminals issue 124
Warsaw 116
Weizsäcker, Ernst von 101
Weygand, Maxime 38
World War I 1, 55
  peace treaties 4–10, 12–13, 123–4

Y

Yamamoto Isoroku 70
Yamashita Tomoyuki 71–2, 117
Yelnya 57
Yugoslavia 47, 70, 93, 96, 105, 124

Z

Zipper (Operation) 117